Acceptance and Com Skills for Perfectionis High-Achieving Behaviors

This book is essential for those who are prone to high-achieving, self-starting, and perfectionistic actions; people who relentlessly, persistently, and determinedly pursue their dreams, goals, and aspirations; people who hold their high standards, principles, and values close to their heart.

Chapter by chapter, you will learn acceptance and commitment skills to harness the power of perfectionism and high-achieving behaviors while living the life you want to live. You will learn how to be yourself, keep your fears in perspective, and do meaningful things without dwelling for hours on the different ways to make things right, postponing things because they aren't ready, struggling for days with rumination, anxiety and stress, or wrestling periodically with harsh criticisms.

This book will show you how you can give your best, work hard, and push yourself when you deeply care about things without sacrificing your well-being, hurting your relationships, or compromising your health. You will learn when to engage in high-achieving actions in an effective, life-expansive, and skillful way. You will develop a new workable relationship with all those narratives about not being good enough and treat yourself with kindness, compassion, and caring. Most importantly, you will find that you can be yourself without losing yourself.

Patricia E. Zurita Ona, Psy.D., "Dr. Z.," is a psychologist specializing in working with and creating compassionate, research-based, and actionable resources for overachievers and overthinkers to get them unstuck from worries, fears, anxieties, perfectionism, procrastination, obsessions, and ineffective playing-it-safe actions.

Dr. Z. is the founder of the East Bay Behavior Therapy Center, a boutique practice, where she offers therapy and coaching services based on acceptance and commitment therapy (ACT) and contextual behavioral science. Dr. Z. has been nominated a Fellow of the Association of Contextual Behavioral Science because of her contributions to the applications of ACT to specific fear-based struggles.

"This book is an incredible resource for anyone struggling to balance their drive for high achievement with their wellbeing and relationships. Underpinned by behavioral science, Dr. Z. invites you to consider when to follow perfectionistic actions and when to disentangle from them. She shows you chapter by chapter how to play the workability game while building a fulfilling life. This is my go-to text for any person that wants to learn how to make their high standards work for them over the long term."
—**Jonny Say**, ACT and Compassionate-focused Therapist

"This fabulous book teaches you how to live a vital and meaningful life while pursuing the high standards that you find important and without losing yourself in the process. Using Acceptance and Commitment skills, Dr. Z. provides you with a compassionate frame to make sense of your perfectionistic actions, keep them in check, and do what works. You will learn to lean into your values and make room for anxieties and fears of being a failure, without losing your drive to achieve."
—**Kim Rockwell-Evans**, Ph.D., OCD and Anxiety Specialists of Dallas

"In a relatable, compassionate, and clear way, Dr. Z. deconstructs a complex topic. Grounded in acceptance and commitment therapy (ACT), she guides you through the nuances of perfectionism and teaches you how to go beyond the labels of good and bad or right and wrong, so you can create a values-driven and workable relationship with perfectionistic actions. A must read for anyone that wants to harness the power of high achieving actions while living a fulfilling life!"
—**Michael Heady**, LCPC; Co-Director of the Anxiety and Stress Disorders Institute of Maryland

"This book is vital for anyone who has wrestled with holding themselves to high personal standards while at the same time drowning in the overwork and overwhelm that such high standards bring. It's a practical guide that digs into why it's so hard for high-achievers to step back and let go, and how to embrace progress over perfection to live a calmer, less anxious, and happier life. It's a book that I will absolutely recommend to all of my self-confessed perfectionist clients, colleagues, and friends."
—**Ellen Jackson**, Workplace and Coaching Psychologist, Podcaster

"If you're suffering from the chronic stress and strain of perfectionism, help is at hand. But this not just any old help. This is wise, practical, realistic help, based not on pop psychology, but solid science. Within these pages, Patricia Zurita Ona will guide you, with great wisdom and compassion, in breaking free from the shackles of perfectionism, and building a life of freedom and fulfilment. You're in good hands. Enjoy the journey."
—**Russ Harris**, Author of *The Happiness Trap*

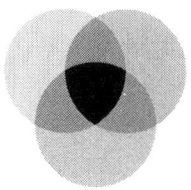

Acceptance and Commitment Skills for Perfectionism and High-Achieving Behaviors

Do Things Your Way, Be Yourself, and Live a Purposeful Life

PATRICIA E. ZURITA ONA, PSY.D.

NEW YORK AND LONDON

First published 2022
by Routledge
605 Third Avenue, New York, NY 10158

and by Routledge
4 Park Square, Milton Park, Abingdon, Oxon, OX14 4RN

Routledge is an imprint of the Taylor & Francis Group, an informa business

© 2022 Taylor & Francis

The right of Patricia E. Zurita Ona to be identified as author of this work has been asserted in accordance with sections 77 and 78 of the Copyright, Designs and Patents Act 1988.

All rights reserved. No part of this book may be reprinted or reproduced or utilised in any form or by any electronic, mechanical, or other means, now known or hereafter invented, including photocopying and recording, or in any information storage or retrieval system, without permission in writing from the publishers.

Trademark notice: Product or corporate names may be trademarks or registered trademarks, and are used only for identification and explanation without intent to infringe.

Library of Congress Cataloging-in-Publication Data
A catalog record for this book has been requested

ISBN: 978-0-367-36919-4 (hbk)
ISBN: 978-0-367-36922-4 (pbk)
ISBN: 978-1-003-08315-3 (ebk)

DOI: 10.4324/9781003083153

Typeset in Lato
by Apex CoVantage, LLC

I would like to dedicate this book to my mother, Patricia.
I'm grateful for everything you have taught me about humbleness and constant love.

DOWNLOAD THE FREE AUDIO GUIDE

As a thank you for buying this book, I would like to give you an audio guide for it for FREE!!

TO DOWNLOAD GO TO:

https://www.thisisdoctorz.com/act-for-perfectionism-and-high-achieving-behaviors/

Contents

Introduction	1

SECTION I
What's Wrong With Caring Deeply? — 3

  1 Why Bother With This Book? — 5
  2 Doing Things Perfectly Makes Sense! — 8
  3 Others Are Wrong, You're Right — 10
  4 Flipping the Coin — 13
  5 All Types of High-Achieving Actions — 16

SECTION II
Unpacking Your Personal History — 19

  6 How Come You Care So Much? — 21
  7 The Many Shades of Fear — 28
  8 Mistakes, Errors, Flaws — 31
  9 A Special Type of Fear — 34
  10 Mental Rubrics — 37
  11 Personal Narratives — 41

SECTION III
Harnessing the Power of High-Achieving and Perfectionistic Actions — 45

12 The Future of Caring Behaviors — 47

13 What Are Your Precious Values? — 49

14 Does It Really Matter? — 55

15 Important Questions, Important Answers — 57

16 One Year From Now — 59

17 "Doing Things Right" Is the Right Thing to Do, at Times — 62

18 What Game Are You Playing? — 65

SECTION IV
The Workability Game — 67

19 Learning About It — 69

20 Playing It — 76

21 Committing to It — 79

SECTION V
Pause and Play — 83

22 The Great Escape — 85

23 Fleeting Feelings — 88

24 Seizing and Freezing — 91

25 Overly Protective Friends — 94

26 To Buy or Not to Buy? — 96

27 Hold Them Lightly, Really! — 98

28	99 Percent	100
29	This-Or-That Thoughts	103
30	Minding and Unwinding	105
31	Mini-Me Stories	108
32	Terrible Feelings	111
33	Pleased to Meet You!	113
34	Plus and Minus	115
35	Don't Go Down the Rabbit Hole!	118
36	Daring to Be Kind!	120
37	Vulnerabilities or Liabilities?	123
38	Less Chasing, More Choosing	126
39	When-Then Thoughts	129
40	Tough Choices Need Kindness	132

SECTION VI
Onward and Upward! — **135**

41	Messy Moments	137
42	Living With Not Knowing	139
43	Undoing Decidophobia	142
44	Tackling Procrastination	145
45	Tough Love!	148
46	Let's Move	150
47	To Quit or Not to Quit	153

48	Finding Your Rhythm	157
49	Little Tidbits	161
50	Sweet Contradictions	165
51	Sugarcoating Moments	167
52	O-VER-RE-SPON-SI-BIL-I-TY	170
53	Doing Less, Living More	173
	Final Words	177

Acknowledgments   179
Appendix   180
   Online Classes With Dr. Z.   180
   Books Written by Dr. Z.   180
   Working With Dr. Z.   180
   Professional Consultation With Dr. Z.   181
   Speaking Engagements With Dr. Z.   181
References   182

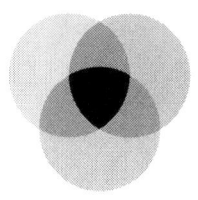

Introduction

This is not a book in which you will read the usual clichés about high-achieving and perfectionistic actions.

This is a book that shows you how to nurture, cultivate, and enrich your drive for high achievement without the sleepless nights, many hours of regret, years of blaming and criticizing yourself, or dwelling relentlessly on worries, fears, or anxieties.

This book is grounded in acceptance and commitment therapy (ACT) and current findings from organizational and social psychology.

I believe – and behavioral science shows – that to create and live the life we want, we need to learn to accept ourselves as we really are, rather than as we wish to be. And if you're prone to being a high achiever and a perfectionist, this book is an invitation to do so.

Wanting to give your best, making the right decisions, and striving to have all the information when something matters to you makes sense, because you care deeply. That's not necessarily the problem; the problem is when these behaviors go unchecked, take on lives of their own, and become more debilitating than fulfilling.

I invite you to place this book on your coffee table, on your night table, in your bag or purse, or in any other location where you might see it often, to make it easy for you to grab and read it – and, most important, for you to practice all the new skills you'll learn in these pages.

One last thing: finding your way to the life you want is a major undertaking, so instead of rushing through these pages, pace yourself. Reflect on what you read, put into action what you learn, be curious about what you discover, and take the time to appreciate the work you're doing.

Kindly,

Dr. Z.

(*) P.S. Remember to download the free audio guide: https://www.thisisdoctorz.com/act-for-perfectionism-and-high-achieving-behaviors/

DOI: 10.4324/9781003083153-1

Section I

What's Wrong With Caring Deeply?

I feel judged because I'm passionate. I feel judged because I want to thrive. I feel judged because I want to give my best. I feel judged because I always have something going on.

People think that I do things because I want to be rich or famous.

I have felt unseen hundreds of times . . . It's the story of my life . . . few people get my passions, my fears, my anxieties . . . and the things that truly move me.

I'm often asked the question, when are you going to stop doing this . . . ? People don't get how much that question hurts me at times. People don't know how it feels to be misunderstood. People don't know how it feels to be unseen. People don't know that . . . I won't ever change. This is my essence.

Anonymous

1 Why Bother With This Book?

Hello and welcome to *Acceptance and Commitment Skills for Perfectionism and High-Achieving Behaviors: Do Things Your Way, Be Yourself, and Live a Purposeful Life*!

Before you start reading this book, I have some questions for you:

- Do you strive to do your best, no matter what you're working on?
- Do you pay attention to details and aim for quality when you're doing something important to you?
- Do you spend extra time making sure that you're saying the right thing, doing the right thing, and acting the right way?
- Do you sometimes postpone decisions or tasks because you want to make the optimal choice?
- Do you avoid starting things until you're sure you have all the necessary information?
- Do you hold yourself responsible for others' well-being to the point that every choice you make must be a true reflection of your character?
- Do you struggle when others appear to be careless with things that are important to you?
- Do you know how it feels when working hard, paying attention to detail, and giving your best pays off?
- Do you appreciate the struggles, sweat, and tribulations that go into getting things right?
- Are you familiar with that feeling that comes when you've said the right thing, done the right thing, and acted in the right way in a given situation?

If you answered yes to any of these questions, you're reading the right book.

This is a book for people who pursue excellence, deal regularly with harsh self-criticism, and feel a strong sense of responsibility for every decision they make.

This is a book for people who want to do things the right way, who care about the details, and who worry about making mistakes.

DOI: 10.4324/9781003083153-3

This is a book for people who are prone to high-achieving, go-getting, self-starting, and perfectionistic actions.

This is a book for people who relentlessly, persistently, and determinedly pursue their dreams, goals, and aspirations.

This is a book for people who hold their high standards, principles, and values close to their heart.

This is a book for people who are passionate about certain causes, committed to personal values, and dedicated to doing meaningful things.

Giving our best, working hard, and pushing ourselves make total sense when we're doing something important, something we're invested in, and something we care deeply about. It can be very invigorating, refreshing, and exciting.

I know firsthand how it feels to spend hours thinking and thinking about an idea for a project – envisioning it, dreaming about it, chatting about it with others, and making it happen. It's a very special feeling. I personally wouldn't trade it for anything.

But let's step back for a moment and think about what else comes along with working super hard to accomplish an outcome that reflects who you are.

There is usually a lot more going on than what meets the eye. What is happening behind the scenes?

Perhaps you spend too many hours dwelling on the different ways to make something just right, postpone things because they aren't ready, look carefully at every detail, and make sure your standards are reflected.

You probably worry about disappointing others. When this happens, you are unable to sleep at times, forget to eat, feel anxious about failing, and work without stopping because you need to get something done in just the right way.

Chances are you feel despair when things don't go as expected, that you become frustrated when others don't do things right, and that you are harsh with yourself when the outcome isn't what you had in mind.

It's possible that you've been told that you're a perfectionist, or that you're too perfectionistic, or that you fixate on details. You may have been warned that you worry too much about how things are, how you're communicating with others, or how you're completing a project.

People may have told you, "You look great," or "It was so good to see you," and yet, you can't stop feeling concerned about how you looked in those pants or whether you used a harsh tone when you spoke to your friend at dinner the night before.

Or maybe you're like me and enjoy savoring beautiful things. As a person who loves typography, I genuinely appreciate how typography can make a document look clean, elegant, and soothing to the eye. When I'm reading a document, I quickly notice typographical subtleties: multiple fonts, various font sizes, the space between paragraphs, the space between the header and the footer. To be honest, it sometimes hurts my eyes. I have even asked people I work with to please not send me documents with mixed typography. It drives me nuts! I don't get why other people aren't bothered by messy-looking things in the same way I'm bothered by it!

Do any of these situations speak to you? If so, once again, you're reading the right book!

Don't worry, this book won't tell you to stop putting all your enthusiasm into creating excellent projects, growing in your career, or caring for others. These pages won't tell you to be less responsible for others' well-being, to be less accountable for what you do, or to live with less-high standards.

Chapter by chapter, I'll share with you how to harness the power of high-achieving and perfectionistic actions while living the life you want to live. I'll show you how you can keep pushing yourself and maintaining high standards without sacrificing your well-being, hurting your relationships, or being self-critical.

My approach is to expand on what you're already doing effectively, teach you to feel proud of your accomplishments, and coach you on how to do these things yourself so you can build a rich, fulfilling, and meaningful life!(*) P.S. Remember to download the free audio guide: https://www.thisisdoctorz.com/act-for-perfectionism-and-high-achieving-behaviors/

2 Doing Things Perfectly Makes Sense!

Rick Barry, a former American professional basketball player, is famous for shooting free throws almost to perfection. Free throws, or foul shots, are taken from 15 feet away from a ten-foot-tall hoop. The shot seems simple, yet most professional basketball players are successful less than 75 percent of the time. If you follow basketball, you may know that Barry is a legend – and an admitted perfectionist – who is proud to say that he views 90 percent free-throw success as the minimum standard. He publicly admitted getting upset when others don't work hard to improve their free throws and can easily go to sleep without struggling with their performance (Fixler, 2012).

I'm wondering if Rick Barry should be reading this book. Who knows? But here are my questions for you: do you relate to Barry's agony in not understanding why people wouldn't strive to be the best at what they do? Do you wonder how people can possibly find peace or purpose when not accomplishing perfection?

When I'm working on a manuscript, for example, I spend hours and hours studying a topic: reading journal articles, newspaper articles, and blogs; listening to podcasts; bothering my friends with research questions; piloting exercises with my clients; scribbling thoughts on sticky notes; and pondering the best ways to convey an idea. So when I see some of my psychology students doing the bare minimum – investing the tiniest amount of time conducting research for their dissertation projects or writing the shortest report possible – I genuinely have to breathe slowly: I don't get why they don't care about the quality of their work. Since when is doing the minimum amount okay?

How is it for you? How often do you have thoughts like Barry? How often do you become frustrated when others don't put their best effort into the work they're doing, don't strive for maximizing a process, or don't pay attention to how they're coming across?

Can you think of a situation when you were surprised by the lack of interest others showed in something you really cared about? How did that feel?

You're not alone. You're a high achiever. You are part of a group of individuals who strive to do things right, who want to do things better

DOI: 10.4324/9781003083153-4

and better, who have determination to do things with high standards, who have a natural overdrive, and who feel often misunderstood by others.

The truth is that, when doing what's important to you, it's natural to want to do it right, to the best of your ability, and with great care. This makes complete sense. There is nothing wrong with you for thinking this way.

You just need to learn how to effectively handle – without losing yourself, your standards, and your sense of what's important – those moments when the world around you doesn't care as much about certain things as you do.

Others Are Wrong, You're Right

"You should let it go."
"You're worrying too much about the details."
"People don't take things as seriously as you do; just ignore those mistakes."
"Oh, just forget about it."
"Don't focus on the minutiae, but on the big picture."
"There will always be mistakes."
"You should chill; things will work out either way."

How many times have you heard these messages? My bet is that if you were given a piece of chocolate every time someone made a comment like that, you would be opening your chocolate store by now. Right? Quite likely, you have heard these comments hundreds, if not thousands, of times in books, in social media posts, in workshops, or from friends and others around you. They advise you to lower your standards, do less, let go of perfection, and on and on.

Pause for a moment and check in with yourself. How does it feel when others ask you to lower your standards? Do you know how to do that? Do you want to do that? Do you ever follow their advice? Does it make you think twice about what you're doing and how you're living? What happens when people tell you to "just let it go"? Do you change yourself and your actions based on these remarks?

But I Always Have to Do My Best!

Let me introduce you to Rebecca. She is very passionate about playing tennis competitively. She practices every other day, follows a specific workout routine, and watches her favorite players' matches on repeat. She also pushes herself to get straight As in all her classes at school.

One day, when we are discussing her week, we stop to do some rough calculations to determine how many hours a week she needs to complete all the things she needs to do; the number we come up with is 112. It becomes clear that things need to be removed from her plate. When I ask her to consider what she can give up for that week, she looks at me, eyes open wide, eyebrows raised, as if I had killed someone, and says,

DOI: 10.4324/9781003083153-5

Others Are Wrong, You're Right 11

"Doctor Z, why should I not work hard at the things I do? Why shouldn't I give them my best? Are you asking me to do things halfway?"

Rebecca is not the only person who's asked me this question or variations of it. I've heard a multitude of responses from the many people I've worked with. All of their responses are very real and consistent with their view of things.

"Stop being a perfectionist! Stop being a high achiever! Stop caring so much!"

Most of my clients are annoyed with advice like this, whether it comes from relatives, books, coaches, or even therapists. It's easy for people to tell you to stop this or that. It's easy to preach about how you should just let things go. And yet, you and I know that it's not easy to drop things when you deeply care about them.

I know in my heart that if it were this easy-peasy for my clients to change their behaviors, to stop caring as much as they do, they would have done it a long time ago.

Maybe you've tried to do things differently. Maybe you tried to ignore the possibility of things going wrong with a work project. Maybe you tried not to tell your partner that the desk she wants to buy is not the best one. Maybe you have done your utmost to turn in a paper without reading all the publications on the topic. Maybe you tried to apply for a job without reading the application form over and over. Maybe you tried to finish writing a paper without working until 2 a.m. every night. Maybe you tried to discuss something with your in-laws without rehearsing it in your head hundreds of times. Maybe you tried to go out without wearing that shirt that hides the imperfect areas of your stomach.

The challenge is that each attempt to let things go gives rise to unpleasant thoughts and feelings that pull you into a rabbit hole of confusion, doubt, and distress – and hours of wondering how you can let go of something that matters to you.

The truth is that it's hard to stop doing things that you have grown accustomed to doing, things that often work in your favor. And it's also hard to repeatedly hear these one-size-fits-all messages that never seem to work for you.

None of these phrases ring true to a person who is very invested in doing things perfectly. If I were in your shoes – and I have been, many times – these comments would make me feel unseen and annoyed. They would go in one ear and out the other. I would feel misunderstood and pushed to behave in a way that is not consistent with who I am and how I want to be.

But presumably, if you're reading this book, you do want to change something in your life.

So, the key questions for you are:

- How can I get things done, and to my exacting standards, without wrestling with the distress, anxiety, fear, and annoying thoughts about my performance?

- What research-based skills do I need to learn to live the life I want to live, doing the things I care about, without spending hours at night worrying about messing up a project or making a catastrophic mistake? How do I deal with a rabbit hole of details that goes everywhere but leads nowhere?

With this book, I invite you to maximize, capitalize on, and even augment all those efforts to do the things you care about while enriching, expanding, and making the best of your life. The goal is to get you to a point where you're still achieving and excelling, *and* you aren't compromising other areas of your life. Super cool, right?

4 Flipping the Coin

What leads you to spend hours and hours thinking and thinking about what you're working on?
Why do you pay such careful attention to the nitty-gritty of the things or situations you're interested in?
What makes it hard for you to let go of some things, some standards, or some preferences?
Why does your mind keep turning situations over and over when you are supposed to fall asleep?
What makes you push yourself harder and harder, only allowing yourself to take a break when things are done?
What leads you to keep going even when others around you are telling you to stop, to let things go, or to drop things altogether?
How come you wrestle with the possibility of failing?
What makes you so critical of yourself?
What makes you feel responsible for others' feelings, emotions, and well-being?

Do you ever wonder why others don't care as much about the things they're participating in, about how they come across in a conversation, or about the quality of their work? Do you find yourself amazed by how others don't feel as concerned about the impact of their decisions as you do about yours?

In this chapter, we're going to unpack what truly drives those behaviors so you can decide what to do about them.

Think for a moment of three situations in three different areas of your life – work, school, parenting, partnership, religion, sports, health, or any others – that went south and were far from ideal.

Think about the specifics: what went wrong? How did you feel about the situations and yourself? To guide you in this reflection, consider the following questions for each situation:

- How bothered, frustrated, or annoyed were you by the situation?
- How much were you able to focus on other projects afterward?
- How did you respond to others' behaviors in regard to this situation?

DOI: 10.4324/9781003083153-6

14   What's Wrong With Caring Deeply?

- How did you treat yourself?
- What did you think of yourself?

Before we analyze your responses, let's meet Reddish. He's a paralegal, father of three, and committed to being the best father he could possibly be. Lately, Reddish has been concerned about one of his kids, Tim, getting into fights at school.

While at work, Reddish finds himself filling his mind with thoughts about the right way to address Tim's behaviors. Reddish is afraid that Tim's misbehaviors will continue, worsen, and ultimately make Tim a troubled teen.

Driven by these thoughts, Reddish calls his partner, shares his worries, and demands that they do something about Tim's behavior. His partner explains that they are already doing what they can, reminds Reddish that Tim is in therapy, and shares his hope that, with time, they will figure out how to handle this situation.

Reddish gets more upset and hangs up on his partner. He can't make sense of why his partner doesn't seem to worry about their son's problems. He wonders what kind of parent he is and how he can be so relaxed and calm about the situation.

Reddish decides to contact other people who might help. He sends emails asking for advice on which books to read, for child therapist recommendations, for boarding schools, and for referrals for family therapy. He also requests regular meetings with Tim's teacher for the next six months.

By lunchtime, Reddish hasn't reviewed any of the contracts that are on his desk, feels stressed about it, and doesn't know what to say to his manager. He requests an extension to finish reviewing them but is denied; he doesn't have a choice but to stay until very late to get the work done.

Reddish is scared about Tim's future, frustrated with his partner's response, feeling like he's failing as a father, exhausted by all the work he has to do in too-few hours, and worries about this delay being reflected in his evaluation.

What's *Really* Important to You?

Now, after considering your three different situations, imagine each one as one side of a coin. Now, imagine that the other side of the coin is your response to the question: what hurts the most about that situation?

Take a moment to reflect on what's behind each one of the situations. What really drives your actions for each one?

When Reddish considers these questions, he notices that what hurts him the most is the possibility of Tim not having a good life. When asking himself, once again, what makes it so painful for him, he notices that he is upset with himself for not being able to protect Tim as he feels he should, as his father. Reddish also notices how ashamed he feels about the possibility of not being able to guide his son.

What did you learn about each one of your situations when flipping the coin and seeing what's on the other side? This reflection may not be easy at first, but I encourage you to keep asking yourself these questions:

- What really hurts about this situation?
- What's truly important for me here?

My experience has been that behind these things that bother us – these things that others say are "wrong," things that we're told are "imperfect" – is the stuff that is really important to us.

Is it possible that the more you care about something, the more you open yourself to struggle?

Is it possible that when you struggle to pay attention to all of the details, push yourself so hard, or spend hours thinking and thinking about a situation, you do so because you genuinely care about it?

Is it possible that you spend hours at bedtime worrying about a situation, criticizing yourself harshly, or agonizing about making the best decisions simply because you care deeply about what you're doing and have the best intentions for it?

When you care about something, you go out of your way to make it excellent. You do your best to stay on track and strive for zero mistakes. It all makes sense: you want to do things perfectly because you care.

But if you are reading this book, it's because you care about so many things that you realize you can't give everything and everyone equal attention. In other words, some parts of your life are suffering, and you want to change that. Perhaps your relationship is in trouble, your health is deteriorating, you're feeling lonely, someone has rejected you, you're feeling burned out, or you're tired of trying so hard.

The problem, my friend, is not that you care deeply. The problem is that you're going about doing the things you care about in a way that's no longer working for you.

5 All Types of High-Achieving Actions

No matter how perfectionistic behaviors look, sound, or feel – or how they developed – they're all driven by what you care about, what deeply matters to you, and what speaks to you. It just happens that when these actions go unchecked, they can easily become a terrible headache to you, add unnecessary pain to your week, and cause you to doubt who you are.

Throughout your life you've had thousands of experiences that have shown you what you care about. In this chapter, you will review the areas of your life in which you push yourself really hard, struggle with failing, and have a hard time letting go of.

Here is a list of areas that most people care about; you may care deeply about all of them or some of them more than others.

- Work ethic, integrity, and moral matters
- Social performance, including conversations and presentations
- Sports, athletics, and fitness
- Career accomplishments
- Academic performance
- Religion or spirituality
- Leisure
- Eating routines
- Parenting
- Friendships
- Physical appearance
- Any other areas?

Now, identify three areas that you care a lot about. Mentally recall all the concerns you've had about failing others, being a failure, or things going wrong in one form or another in each of the areas.

Let's look at the three areas that Idly, a lighting engineer, identifies as caring deeply about: friendships, eating behaviors, and career accomplishments. She wrote the following:

> Area: Friendships
>
> > I struggle to say no to my friends when they need me because I'm afraid of coming across as selfish. When my friend Geri told

DOI: 10.4324/9781003083153-7

me that she was taking a road trip and asked me to take care of her cat, I knew that I shouldn't do it because I was already overextended with chores, grad school commitments, and taking care of a sick uncle. Plus, I needed to exercise. But in that moment, I just couldn't say no and went along with it. I ended up exhausted for two weeks, became a couch potato every night, didn't want to talk to anybody, and felt upset with myself and angry with Geri for asking me to take care of her kitty.

Area: Eating Behaviors

As an adult, I've always wanted to eat healthily. I prefer to eat organic produce and don't like to consume carbs or sugary, high-cholesterol, or highly processed foods. When people invite me to eat at their homes, I usually bring my own food, which means that I always have to make extra time for cooking and feel very stressed if I don't do so. If people invite me to eat out, I usually list some of the five restaurants where I allow myself to eat because their food is clean, healthy, and fresh. I never get dessert, don't drink cocktails, and don't consume anything if I don't know its nutritional composition.

One time, I went on a date, and my date suggested we grab pizza. I was reluctant to do so but felt curious about this person and decided to go along with the plan. Once at the pizzeria, though, I decided I wasn't going to eat anything – not even a salad – and was going to drink tea instead. He clearly noticed my discomfort and asked me if everything was okay. I kept saying yes, but my stress about the food situation was evident. I remember trying to chat with him, but he kept saying how weird it was for him to be eating alone with somebody at the same table. We never saw each other again.

Area: Career Accomplishments

When editing the lighting of a movie, I'm very focused on soft lighting and backlighting, and I have to play with degrees of light and dark, carefully creating the tone for different scenes in a way that makes it more artistic, real, and appealing to the eyes of the viewers. I love my job, but it also bothers me that, many times, I can't let go of details and have to postpone deadlines because the work's not ready – even though my team of peers tells me it's okay. I wish I didn't get so stuck on these details, but to me they matter so much because I want the lighting to enhance the quality of the film.

Your turn.

Most people believe that perfectionism only relates to careers, academics, sports, or art. That's a myth. Being a go-getter, a high achiever, a self-starter, a perfectionist, or a doer means that you care deeply, and you may do a loooooooooot of things to meet your standards in many areas of your day-to-day life. Perfectionistic actions can morph into every facet of your everyday life. They can show up as people-pleasing actions, pursuing emotional clarity at all times, denying gray areas when looking at moral issues, cooking only your favorite recipes, following rigid routines when completing domestic tasks, or researching relentlessly for the best vacation experience.

In fact, research consistently shows that perfectionistic actions can manifest in many ways (Flett, Greene, & Hewitt, 2004; Hewitt & Flett, 1993; Besser, Flett, & Hewitt, 2010). And that's why you may have seen books for different types of perfectionism: social, academic, career, moral, and more. Also, if you have been to therapy, you may have heard similar terms or variations on perfectionistic behaviors.

The challenge with having a specific category for each form of high-achieving action or area of your life in which they occur is that books, talks, and workshops simply cannot address the hundreds of forms perfectionism can take; they will always be behind. High-achieving actions are like the infinite shades a color could have; the shades may look different, but the color base is always the same. At the end of the day, even though perfectionism may show up in a variety of different ways, what fuels perfectionism at its core is the same for all types.

You don't need to read a book or take a class for each type of high-achieving action you do; instead, you can learn key skills that apply to all of them. That's what acceptance and commitment therapy (ACT) offers you!

All high-achieving behaviors can be nourished, cultivated, and managed with practical, applicable, and actionable ACT skills. Pretty amazing, right?

Section II

Unpacking Your Personal History

If your mind is like mine, you may be pondering, why am I prone to high-achieving actions and perfectionistic behaviors? How did I learn these qualities? Why do I push myself so hard when doing things that are important to me? Why do I keep trying to do things right and perfect when I know that achieving perfection is impossible?

Our wonderful minds need to make sense of who we are and how we become who we are today. The chapters in this section offer you responses to these questions. Page by page, you will explore the different layers that led you to strive to give your best, minimize mistakes, and avoid failure when you care deeply about something.

Some things in these pages may be new to you, others might be familiar, and still others might confirm what you already know.

By the end of this section, you will fully understand how one thing led to another, how these behaviors first began, how they showed up in your day-to-day life, and, most importantly, what keeps them going. Super cool, right?

Here is the deal: you cannot effectively manage the negative stuff that comes with perfectionistic actions if you don't know how they work and how they keep you stuck. And one more thing: it's easy to be harsh with yourself, blame yourself, or criticize yourself; yet, no behavior can be understood without a context. Your personal history is part of your context.

The more you step back and check what drives your high-achieving behaviors, the more prepared you'll be to build a satisfying life – one in which you strive to be your best without the unnecessary waterfall of worry thoughts, excessive hours of research, embarrassment over missed deadlines, or feelings of inadequacy.

Let's dive in!

How Come You Care So Much?

How come you feel such a sense of responsibility about certain things and others don't move a hair on you?
How did you learn to push yourself hard with some things but be so relaxed about other things?
How did you learn to care so deeply about others that you feel ultra-responsible for their feelings?
How did you develop this mindset that rigorously fosters growth, effort, and a commitment to what you do?

At different times in your life, when something went wrong with the things or the people you care about, you may have wondered how you became who you are, how you became fond of high-achieving and perfectionistic actions. Other times, you may have quickly blamed, criticized, or condemned yourself. You may have immediately questioned your character, abilities, or integrity. But the fact is that none of us became who we are today without being connected to our past, memories, dreams, fears, and life experiences.

In this chapter, I'll walk you through different variables that will hopefully give you a deeper understanding of what started your perfectionistic actions, what keeps them going, and how you can make sense of them. Of course, I don't know the Truth with a capital "T" about what led you to care soooo deeply about certain things, but I do know that by guiding you on your own investigation, I can invite you to discover for yourself how each one of these variables relates to your unique experience.

Let's begin.

We're Wired to Experience Fear, Anxiety, and Worry

Thousands of years ago, our ancestors endured and survived life-threatening weather conditions, petrifying predators, scarcity of food, relentless enemies, unknown diseases, and many more extremely harsh situations. How do you think they felt in those moments?

Quite likely they felt a spectrum of fear-based emotions: worry, dread, panic, fear, anxiety, terror, and so on. How might it have been if they weren't vigilant about their enemies attacking? What could

DOI: 10.4324/9781003083153-9

have happened if they weren't concerned about their strength to carry their children? How might things have turned out if they weren't worried about having enough water?

If they didn't experience any of those fear-based emotions, they couldn't have made it very far. Their fear-based emotions pushed them to protect themselves in one way or another and kept them alive. Our ancestors experienced those feelings then, and because of evolution we're wired to experience them today, even though we're living in a very different environment.

We Evolved to Be Afraid of Failing

Have you ever imagined what might have happened if a cavewoman confused the sound of a wild animal with a docile one? If a caveman had confused his enemies with his friends? If a clan chose a poor location for a settlement and ran out of water? The price for their mistakes would have meant serious injuries, illnesses, or death.

The cavemen and cavewomen were not only predisposed to experience fear-based emotions, but to develop extremely careful behaviors to prevent mistakes, failing, or doing the wrong things. They survived by learning to be afraid of errors, slips, and mishaps. Because of evolution, our brains do exactly the same these days.

These days when worrying about dropping the ball – given that we're wired to experience all types of fear-based emotions and that our brains have learned to be vigilant to the possibility of failing – we may do various things to prevent it.

Unfortunately, every attempt to prevent a mistake ends up strengthening a pattern of responses that feeds into our fear of making mistakes. In other words, what we do to avoid our fear coming true can actually make that fear stronger. Bear with me for a little bit as I explain.

Think of Rebecca for a moment. When Rebecca was in second grade, she was afraid of doing poorly in math. Sometimes the teacher would ask a student to solve a problem in front of the class, and if that child got the answer wrong, it was with everyone's eyes on them. Rebecca hated that.

To prepare for a math test, Rebecca lined up her special colored pencils next to her notebook, completed one math problem after another, and asked her mom to test her multiple times on different addition and subtraction problems. When the time came, she completed the math test almost to perfection, but when she received her score, she realized she'd made a mistake. Rebecca started crying. She couldn't stop herself. Even though everyone around her told her that she'd only missed one question, she couldn't let it go. After Rebecca sobbed for an hour straight, the teacher called her mom. Rebecca explained what happened and continued crying at home until midafternoon. No matter what her mom said, Rebecca was still hurting because of that mistake.

As Rebecca progressed academically, her fear of making mistakes unfolded in other ways. She became concerned about making mistakes in her spelling class, so as a preventive measure, she made 200 flash cards and asked everyone to test her.

Rebecca also became fearful about not being liked by her friends, so she always tried to say the right things to them. Rebecca got concerned about her weight and body shape, so she weighed herself, stared at herself in the mirror, and measured her body fat daily. When starting to date, Rebecca became preoccupied with not being as attractive as her friends, so she often asked her friends how many dates they had and compared herself to them. When having her friends over for dinner, Rebecca couldn't stop feeling afraid of being a bad host so she repeatedly asked her friends if the food was okay.

Over time, Rebecca figured out that if she learned to prepare, check, and meticulously pay attention to things, she could prevent bad situations from happening; and with every new fear, she continued to do the same. And every action she took reinforced her need to minimize the possibility of making a mistake, of things going wrong, or of failing.

You May Have a Predisposition to Experience Negative Emotional States

The general tendency to experience negative emotional states is called *neuroticism*. It is considered one of the "big five" factors of personality (Costa, 1993) and is experienced generally on a continuum. For instance, a person who worries about things going wrong, has mood shifts, gets easily irritated, and perceives things generally negatively or as indicators of future disaster may rank high for neuroticism, because this person is more often than not in a negative emotional state.

When Charlie, an architect, received news that his main client would be in town, his thoughts about all the things that could go wrong began to spiral. He worried that the plans wouldn't be ready in time or would have mistakes. And if his client found an error in the plans, he might break the contract, file a complaint against him, and possibly even advise others not to work with Charlie's company. Charlie worried that his career and entire livelihood was at stake.

Even though the client would not be arriving for a few weeks, Charlie immediately began work on the plans. At home, after having dinner with his family, Charlie spent hours in his home office reviewing different details of the plans; he stayed up late and woke up in a rush the following day.

Getting hooked on thoughts like these from time to time is one thing, but regularly perceiving situations in this way is more in line with having a high level of neuroticism.

Your Parents or Caregivers May Have Instilled Expectations About How to Do Things

Alice's parents were both teachers, and they often encouraged Alice and her brother to be the best at everything they did so they could have solid futures. Alice remembers that when she would do the dishes, she would get advice from her father about how to wash them correctly; she received many tips about the best ways to complete a puzzle, read a story, fold clothes, be nice to others, and make spaghetti.

Alice wasn't as detail-oriented as her dad, so sometimes she would miss one thing or another, and then she would watch as her father reacted with confusion, dissatisfaction, and concern. Her father never screamed or punished her; he even tried to be silly at times when giving her feedback. But Alice knew when he was disappointed by what she'd done. Alice knew that her father would feel proud of her when she pushed herself really hard to achieve the best outcome in anything she participated in.

Maybe prominent adults in your life set expectations for you. Maybe they pushed you to always perform your best, to study or work hard, to practice over and over until you got something right. Maybe they constantly told you the "right" ways of doing thing. And maybe you were punished when you didn't do your best or when you did things "wrong."

You Watched Others Do Things Right and Perfectly

Sometimes my clients confess that their parents, caregivers, or other people they grew up with never told them explicitly about the importance of doing things perfectly or never put pressure on them to be high achievers or to excel at everything they do. But, as we unpack the sources of their beliefs about high-achieving actions, they recall memories of people around them who never missed work even when they were sick, who always did things impeccably, who never lied, who got upset if they made a mistake, who blamed themselves for negative outcomes, or who strived to do things diligently when the stakes were high.

When Reza was growing up, at dinnertime he often heard his parents discuss being upset if another person hadn't shown up for an appointment, had canceled a meeting at the last minute, or had handled a situation poorly. He sometimes heard his father talk about having made a mistake at work, and he would dwell on how he'd failed to pay attention to detail, how he should have known better, and how he felt bad about himself for having made that mistake. Reza recalls how his father took to heart doing the right thing for others, and would not tolerate the idea of being irresponsible, disrespectful, or rude toward others. Reza's dad held high morals and was committed to them.

Reza didn't know how he was relating to those messages; he was just a kid learning from his parents. His struggles started in high school when he became a gymnast. He couldn't understand why his peers didn't want to do better with some of the postures and jumps; he quietly criticized those who were doing the minimum and made sure that he was giving his best at every practice.

Were there adults in your life that may have inadvertently modeled perfectionist or high-achieving behaviors for you? What do you remember noticing about people in your family, community leaders, coaches, teachers, neighbors, or anyone else?

You Learned That a Person's Worth Is Reflected by How Well They Do Things

Kaleb heard loud, explicit, direct messages from his adopted parents about how "good people do things with care, always give their best, and don't measure how hard they work or how much time they spend to get things done; they just get them right."

Only as an adult, when reminiscing about his childhood memories, Kaleb saw how, very early, he had tied his identity and worth to his ability to do well in all things. When he made a mistake, a wrong decision, or didn't do as well as he hoped, he felt that he was was terrible, bad, or a useless person.

You Learned to Rely on Perfectionistic Behaviors to Avoid Uncomfortable Feelings

It's also possible that when your mind comes up with a chain of awful thoughts about you failing, disappointing others, not looking good, or being mediocre, you feel different types of fear-based emotions. Maybe you worry about feeling like a loser. Maybe you are afraid that your loved ones will suffer as a direct result of the decisions you make. Maybe you get anxious about people discovering that you're a fraud. Maybe you feel uneasy about not being a good parent.

To manage all those fear-based emotions, you do everything you can – high-achieving actions – to prevent those bad things from happening. But every preventive step you take is done to feel good in the moment and to feel less stressed, less worried, and less anxious. At the same time, your mind quickly makes a connection between doing things right and avoiding feeling lousy.

For example, Guptha, a store manager, started each work day at 7 a.m., only took a half-hour lunch break, completed all his daily reports following the appropriate protocols, and didn't leave the store until midnight, after most of his employees were gone. His peers would tell him, "You're amazing! I don't know how you do it; you have superpowers." In those moments, Guptha felt appreciated, seen, and validated for his hard work. He was quickly promoted, only six months after being hired. So he told himself, "I've done well, and it's because I work hard." But Guptha didn't share with his coworkers that every night he's inundated with thoughts about all the things he didn't do right at work, how he should have done better, and how there is a part of him that feels like a fraud for being promoted. He didn't share that every day he wanted to do things better and better than the day before because he was afraid of failing and because he didn't know any other way to manage those worries than by working hard. He didn't share that although he had been in a number of relationships, he usually disconnected from potential partners because they wanted to spend more time with him than he felt able to give without it affecting his work performance.

The problem is that even though you may feel good about the incredible things you get done – high-achieving actions like focusing every day on a particular goal, and moving forward in your career – you don't learn how to manage the negative, uncomfortable, or annoying feelings that are a part of life.

You see, it's really unfair to label yourself and your behaviors without understanding your context, your history, your upbringing, and your experiences. Trying to understand your inclination to high-achieving actions and how you may get easily stressed with imperfection, unpredictability, or failure without considering all the influential variables is like simplifying, minimizing, or denying the complexity of being humans.

When you look back at your personal history, some of these variables may relate to you more than others. The reality is that as each variable, or a combination of them, unfolded in your life at different times, your mind developed an architecture of beliefs about how things should be; how others should perceive you; how you should perform on a given task, project, or activity; how important it is to push yourself and to make optimal decisions; and how hard work pays off.

This architecture of beliefs can seem benign, like nothing to worry about, or even helpful because it looks like your personal preferences:

- I prefer to be seen as a good person versus a person without integrity.
- I prefer to do things right the first time.
- If I don't pay attention to the details, I'll fail.
- If I don't do things correctly now, my future will be negatively affected. Anything I do, I try to succeed at. Why bother otherwise?
- What good comes from doing something when we don't give our best?

At the same time, this architecture of beliefs is likely touching, affecting, and influencing other (maybe all) areas of your life in ways that have become second nature for you. It can be driving your social interactions (making sure you leave a particular impression on others or get their approval), moral decisions (doing your best to always act according to your standards and perceiving anything that violates them as a major infraction), friendships (hoping others will see things as you do and demanding at times that they share your worldview), and health (only eating certain types of foods to make sure you have the perfect diet), just to name a few.

None of this is your fault. It's human to organize your behavior given all the experiences you have been exposed to since you were born. High-achieving behaviors don't magically appear one day or after drinking a special wonder tea. Perfectionistic actions are historical, have been reinforced many times throughout different experiences, show up in various ways, and color many areas of your life.

And that's why it is much more courageous to understand your personal history – to uncover the sources of what you learned – and choose how you want to relate to it as you move forward.

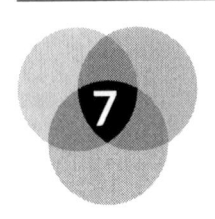

7 The Many Shades of Fear

Scenario 1. I'm walking alone in the street, at night, and I hear the steps of a person running up behind me.
Scenario 2. I'm getting ready to meet my in-laws.
Scenario 3. My friend doesn't return my call, and I think it's possible I hurt her feelings.
Scenario 4. I'm putting a dinner together and trying a new recipe.
Scenario 5. I had a dream in which I'm dying young.
Scenario 6. My kitty didn't leave his bed the whole day.
Scenario 7. I'm going to a vegan restaurant and don't know what type of food I'll be able to eat.

Since the moment we are born and throughout our lives, we experience fear-based emotions of all colors, sizes, and shapes. And, if you strive to do your best when you care about something, then worries, fears, anxieties, and different forms of fear-based emotions are your constant companions.

Fear-based emotions are not pure, precise, or well-defined experiences. Even though most academics distinguish fear as a present-oriented emotion, and anxiety and worry as future-oriented emotions, the reality is that fear-based emotions have maaaaaaany subtleties, and we experience them along a continuum, from the slightest pressure in our chest when we're feeling scared, concerned, or cautious, to a rapidly beating heart when we're feeling dread, panic, or terror.

But, how do you handle fear-based emotions when things matter to you? To start, let's take a look at the messages you received about them from your relatives, caregivers, schools, friends, workmates, and even Slack channels, Facebook groups, and WhatsApp conversations.

- What were you told about how to handle fear? When you were growing up, how did the people around you – parents, caregivers, siblings, other adults in your life – relate to fear?

    Are those messages about handling fear different from or similar to one another? Is there a common theme running through them?

- How do you experience fear in your body? Is there a particular bodily sensation you notice? Is this sensation a static one or does it move?

DOI: 10.4324/9781003083153-10

> Fear-based emotions don't happen just in your head, but also in your body. So, how do you feel them?

- What do you do when you're experiencing a fear based-reaction? What are your go-to ways of handling fear, worries, and anxiety?

  > All of our emotions – all of them – push us to do something, whether to take action, or to do more or less of an activity. What do certain emotions compel you to do or not do?

- If you step back one more time and review the impact of your fear-based emotions on your life, what role do they play? Do they help you? Do they limit you? Do they move you toward being who you want to be?

Both Friend and Foe

Most of us have received countless pieces of advice about fear, as if it's an enemy we need to fight, push down, or ignore. And when something matters to you, you may have also heard messages along the lines of, "You can be fearless, you need to be fearless. To be afraid is to be weak. There is no reason to be afraid. . . ." and so on.

It seems that there is a universal script, with minor variations, that says: fear-based emotions are bad, annoying, uncomfortable, and unnecessary. And naturally, given all that advice, we may quickly judge fear as a bad emotion, go out of our way to minimize, control, or replace it, and feel bad about feeling bad.

For example, if you're afraid of giving a public presentation, you may rehearse it hundreds of times to make sure you got it, you may drink alcohol before your presentation, you may cancel it, or you may spend hours in your head anticipating all the things that could go wrong with it. Some of those actions may make sense and even work at times, but what happens when they take on a life of their own, with the sole purpose of reducing fear?

You see, you will always experience some form, shape, or color of fear-based emotions in your life – that's unavoidable. Experiencing fear is the norm and not the exception for all of us, especially when things are extremely important to us.

As much as we don't like it, fear-based emotions have helped us to survive and have driven very adaptive behaviors many times. Fear can show us what's behind our hurts; for example, when we are rejected, it hurts because there's love there. Fear can motivate us to take effective action; for example, researching different types of loans prepares you to be well informed when buying your first home. Fear can help us to communicate and connect with others; for example, showing empathy to friends struggling with submitting their applications for a new job is comforting. Fear can help us to survive dangerous situations; for example, moving out of the way of a speeding car can save our life.

Fear-based emotions can be our friends, partners, and even supporters when doing what we care about. They can help us to figure out what's going on inside us and what matters. Essentially, they can help us to learn about ourselves, our needs, and what works in a given moment.

So, as you move on with your day and focus on what's important to you, pay attention to the different degrees of fear-based emotions that come your way. See if you can watch them with curious eyes as they occur and not as dictators of your actions. The more aware you are of your fear-based emotions, the more often you can give yourself a chance to choose how to effectively respond to them. And the more energy you will have to do things your way.

8 Mistakes, Errors, Flaws

When Mary is getting ready to submit a research paper, she feels a sense of dread at the possibility of the data not being properly reported, of not having cited all the authors, and of having misrepresented a theory. So, just to make sure there aren't mistakes, she reads the whole paper again, even though she had already read it five times the day before.

The next day, Mary thinks she's done and is ready to submit the paper to her colleague. But when attaching the document to her email, there it is again, the fear of things being incorrectly reported and her reputation crashing because of it. So, she pauses, removes the attachment, prints it out – because she could have missed something by having read it electronically – and reads it again. She feels better, runs to a meeting, and decides she will send the paper the following day.

The following day, Mary wakes up and does her morning routine. But as she is leaving her house, she keeps noticing a sense of concern about the research paper. Despite how many times she's already checked it, she feels a strong fear that there might be mistakes in it.

There are countless things that can be scary for all of us, but there is a particular fear that is unique for high achievers: the fear of making mistakes. This fear is called *atelophobia*.

This fear of making mistakes can be present when talking to others, when making a decision about buying a property, when talking to a date, when choosing the book you're going to read, when doing a job interview, when preparing a movie night with your friends, when searching for patio furniture, or when deciding the hike you want to take on Sunday morning. This is why some of the literature has used terms like "social perfectionism," "moral perfectionism," "existential perfectionism," and many other labels to describe perfectionistic behaviors. But behind all these labels, and many others, is the same basic fear of making mistakes.

When does the fear of making mistakes show up for you? Let's look at different situations you may have encountered. Make a note of which examples apply to you:

DOI: 10.4324/9781003083153-11

_____ When completing a project at home, work, or school

(e.g., doing your best to complete things flawlessly, even with small projects)

_____ When interacting with others

(e.g., making sure you're liked by others)

_____ When making ethical or moral decisions

(e.g., making sure you don't let anyone down or hurt someone)

_____ When dealing with conflict in your relationships
_____ When researching information in preparation for making a decision
_____ When wanting to know how things will be in the future
_____ When parenting your kids, raising them, and teaching them about life
_____ When your peers focus on getting things done instead of looking at how they're done
_____ When considering your diet, exercise, and health
_____ When looking at your appearance, hairstyle, body, and outfits
_____ When making decisions that reflect your morals, ethics, and principles
_____ When others around you don't pay attention to details or forget things

When you are doing things you care about, it's quite likely that you're clear about your intentions. You don't need others to motivate you, remind you about what needs to be done, or check in to see if you're doing the work. It's like you have true north very clearly in your sights. You take steps toward it, have a laser focus, and organize things around it.

But the process of making the things you care about happen is neither straight, clean, nor pain free. In fact, things may go wrong, sometimes terribly wrong.

As one of my former clients said, "It feels really bad to mess things up. It's like I'm a mess. . . . If I drop something, it means that I'm not diligent, that I don't care, that I'm irresponsible."

Your Brain, the Protector

Take a look at your own experience for a moment. Recall a project you really cared about from the past year and identify three challenging moments when things could have gone wrong. Without rushing through these memories, ask yourself, *How does it feel under my skin to go back to those moments when things could have gone south and turned out far from ideal?*

What came up for you?

You may have noticed that when you're doing something you care about, even when you're doing the right thing, there is some amount of distress, discomfort, or worry about things going badly.

Here is what's important to consider: given that you want to do your best because you deeply care about things, and given that what you're participating in or working on comes with all types of possible frustrations, hurts, and disappointments, isn't it natural that your brain would try to protect you from all those potential challenges by demanding that you pay attention to all the things that could go wrong?

Doesn't it make sense that your brain would try to organize your behavior to make sure those potential mistakes don't happen and don't come your way?

The reality is that every time you participate in activities that matter to you, your mind will alert you to potential errors, mistakes, or flaws in one way or another.

Where things get tricky is when you automatically, reactively, and mechanically respond to every possible bad thing that could happen – which is already hard to sit with – and go out of your way to analyze, examine, and scrutinize for more potential disasters.

9 A Special Type of Fear

Who likes to fail? Who wants to fail? Who took the class Failing 101?
Nobody.

It turns out you're not the only one on that track. Of course you don't want to fail, and you do everything you can to avoid failure. As we discussed in Chapter 6, How Come You Care So Much?, we inherited our ancestors' survival strategies, a.k.a. their fear-based emotions. As society evolved, our skills to protect ourselves from failure did too in many sophisticated and complex ways.

Sache, a professional handyman, is proud of the reputation he has for remodeling homes. He loves his job and feels energized by it 24/7. When working on hardwood floors, Sache spends hours and hours aligning and checking and checking again the layout of the many pieces of wood. He ensures they are properly straight and don't have excess glue or nails visible.

His coworkers are usually ready to move into other areas of the remodeling, but Sache tells them, "I need to make it work beautifully and it's not there yet; if I don't get this right, this looks bad on me, as if I'm a careless handyman, and that's not me. I always do my best on every job I have, so you just have to wait for me. I don't want to feel ashamed of my work."

We're often afraid of missing out, being a failure, not doing enough, not being smart enough, being stupid, and on and on. The list of things we could be afraid of is limitless because our human experience is limitless. On top of that, it's possible that you have been encouraged to do your best all the time, to give your best with anything you do, and to have grit, dig deeper, and work harder when something is important to you.

The are many variations of Sache's stories related to the fear of being a failure. One of them goes like this: if you're not always doing your best or being your best, then you're failing, you're not living up to your potential, and you're wasting advantageous attributes.

For high achievers, the fear of failing could easily evolve into a specific phobia – *atychiphobia* – which keeps us stuck and makes us doubt, postpone, and avoid any triggering situation.

Even though the social messages about failure have softened up a bit – for example, more widespread nowadays is the notion that failure

DOI: 10.4324/9781003083153-12

doesn't define you – your mind is not immune to all the messages you receive to avoid failure. So, it's quite possible that you are still holding on to all those thoughts about being a failure.

Let's zoom in on what failure means to you. Here are some questions for you to reflect on:

- When you think of failure, what comes to mind?
- What are all the things you do to avoid failing?
- How do these things work in your life?

Avoiding Failure Is a Win-Lose Behavior

Think of Theresa for a moment. Theresa is a senior data analyst who has worked for large companies throughout her career. As her career progressed, however, she became more and more concerned about being seen as a loser or as stupid by her friends and colleagues. So, she makes a great effort to sound smart, eloquent, and well read when talking to them or presenting information, so that they have a good impression of her decision-making abilities, competence, and proficiency.

To manage her fears of being seeing as stupid or a loser, Theresa has a routine. Each night, she thinks about all the things she has to do the next day. During the day, she often consults with others both inside and outside her company to make sure she's making the right decisions. Theresa searches for the best technological tools so she is always on top of the latest developments, and she drinks scotch before meetings so she sounds more eloquent. As soon as Theresa takes these actions, she feels prepared, secure in her decision, comfortable knowing she looked at all possible options, and much more relaxed around others (after numbing her fears with scotch).

Theresa's strategies to avoid the possibility of failing come in two categories: *public behaviors* – asking others for confirmation and searching for the best tools – and *thinking strategies* – thinking over and over about steps she needs to take, along with considering what-if scenarios. We all do these things, but when you rinse and repeat these actions every time you are afraid of failing or being a failure, you strengthen the habit of doing more and more to feel good temporarily (or at least less badly).

While Theresa benefits from the quick and immediate benefits of each one of these strategies to avoid being a failure, she also struggles with sleeping problems; feeling cranky due to not sleeping well; the stress of missing deadlines and postponing meetings because she isn't 100 percent ready; the mental exhaustion of calling customer service and reading dozens of reviews while searching for the right tools; and the guilt of not making time for her family, exercising regularly, or socializing. A lot of yucky stuff!

Avoiding failure is a win-lose behavior, for real. Each time the fear of failing arises and you get some momentary relief from it by using all those public and private behaviors, the connection between the fear of failing and doing more and more to feel better gets stronger. And of course, as time goes on, your mind will push you to do the same all the time, no matter what the situation is or how much those actions are costing you in your life.

I know it's hard to step back and unpack all your fears about being a failure. Some of the ways you handle your fears may work, others may not; some may be sustainable, others may not be. But not checking how your reactions to being a failure are really impacting your life only perpetuates all the yucky stuff that you don't like.

Imagine, for a moment, what it would look like to stop doing all those things that are not sustainable in the long run and instead use that time, mental energy, and emotional capacity to do the things you enjoy, the things you need to do, and the things you have been neglecting that you care about.

As you finish this chapter, I encourage you to keep an eye on what you do to manage the fear of being a failure. Do you use more public or private behaviors to handle the possibility of failing?

10 Mental Rubrics

Me: Opening my eyes at the beginning of the day.
My mind: Blah blah blah blah blah blah blah blah blah blah blah blah blah blah blah blah blah blah blah blah blah blah blah blah blah blah blah blah blah blah blah blah blah blah blah blah blah blah blah blah blah blah blah blah blah blah.
Me: Sipping a cup of dark roast coffee.
My mind: Blah blah blah blah blah blah blah blah blah blah blah blah blah blah blah blah blah blah blah blah blah blah blah blah blah blah blah blah blah blah blah blah blah blah blah blah blah blah blah blah blah blah blah blah blah blah.
Me: Reading *Blink* by Malcolm Gladwell.
My mind: Blah blah blah blah blah blah blah blah blah blah blah blah blah blah blah blah blah blah blah blah blah blah blah blah blah blah blah blah blah blah blah blah blah blah blah blah blah blah blah blah blah blah blah blah blah blah.

Let's agree that our mind is not a relaxed entity but a busy, hardworking, and super-protective one. Our mind is constantly making sense of anything and everything that's happening inside our skin and outside of it too, without stop. Can you imagine, for a moment, the amount of information we're exposed to and the amount that shows up second by second in our minds?

Not surprising, in order to make sense of all the stuff that shows up in your mind, all the stuff you need to do, and all the stuff you want to do, your mind needs to come up with patterns, configurations, and repetitions of how to make sense of reality. It's impossible to learn to function in the world without having a framework for how to behave.

One of the ways in which our mind creates that framework is by organizing all that input about particular ways of thinking, behaving, and sensing into Rules with a capital "R." Within ACT, we refer to these Rules as *ruling-thoughts* because, at the end of the day, they're just thoughts. They are most certainly special thoughts, though: they're more inflexible, less malleable, and more resistant to change. In this book, I'll use "rules" and "ruling-thoughts" interchangeably.

DOI: 10.4324/9781003083153-13

Some of these ruling-thoughts might be familiar to you and may already be in motion in your mind without you being aware of them. Here are some examples: *pay your bills on time. Look both ways before crossing the street. Don't kill anyone*, and so on. But there are other rules that are so buried and hidden that they go undetected in your day-to-day life; you may not recognize them, but they're directing your actions in the background.

There are three ways to recognize ruling-thoughts:

1. Expressions that include "ought," "should," "must," and "always."

    Juan, a father of three, a public speaker, and a person who exercises every day, thinks:

    - I need to always be available for my kids.
    - A speaker ought to give their audience their best.
    - In order to be fit, I must follow my workout routines perfectly.

2. Overly generalized expectations or preferences for how things should be or how people should behave.

    Tina, a single woman searching for a partner, holds on to thoughts like:

    - I prefer that people text me instead of calling.
    - It's inappropriate for people to have their pets off-leash in a common area.

3. Expressions that include either-or thoughts.

    Rafael, an artist and visual creator, when working, thinks:

    - Every design job matters. Either I come up with a good design for this project or I'm a failed artist.
    - Being late, even once, makes me an unreliable person.

Imagine how many rules our mind comes up with over the course of our existence. Thousands and thousands at least! You may wonder, *What's the purpose of all these thousands of ruling-thoughts?*

Here is the deal: when you care deeply about something, your mind – like a protective bodyguard – will spontaneously come up with all types of rules about how you should perform, how you should get things done, how things will be better if done in a particular way, or how you should respond, feel, or behave in many settings. And your mind does all this with the sole purpose of shielding you from potential disappointments, frustrations, and hurts.

Take a look for yourself: how do you relate to the following ruling-thoughts? While none of these statements is ever completely true or completely false, think about whether you relate to any of them:

- The well-being of the people I love is my responsibility all the time.
- I need to get things right and according to certain standards, otherwise I lose credibility and respect.

- I have to make sure there are no errors when I'm doing something important to me.
- I should make the best decisions possible.
- I should always give my best.
- If I cannot do something right, then it's not worth doing.
- I need to pay attention to details, otherwise there will be mistakes that I'll regret for a long time.
- If I don't put forth my best efforts, I shouldn't expect much in return.
- I shouldn't waste time; that's just bad.
- I need to make sure others are happy and taken care of at all times.

Any other ruling-thoughts that you live by?

Our ruling-thoughts are like mental rubrics – limitless and in every area of our lives, especially when considering our goals, the people we care about, and the things that matter to us.

And, when important things are at stake, and you're prone to high-achieving actions, your mind will develop ruling-thoughts about success, achievement, and accomplishment.

Rulers of Success

What are your thoughts on success? If you glance around, we are bombarded with ideas about what success should look like:

- "No pain, no gain."

    We think about an athlete training multiple hours, being on a strict diet, and possibly becoming injured in order to win.

- "You're successful if you have worked hard and overcome adverse conditions."

    We think about an immigrant who lost his parents and became the CEO of a company.

- "You're living your potential by having a lot of things."

    We think about a software engineer who became a millionaire after his company went public.

- "You're successful if you're being acknowledged by others."

    We think about a Twitter user celebrating having 20K followers.

- "You're accomplished if you feel happy, excited, and bubbly."

    We think about an Instagram user showing all the fun, cute, and happy moments they're living.

How does your mind look at success, achievement, and accomplishments in different areas of your life? What makes you a successful parent? How do you know you're an accomplished professional in your career? How do you know you have succeeded in sports? Think about the different areas of your life – parenting, career, appearance, weight, academics, spirituality, morality, and relationships – and see if you recognize ruling-thoughts in those areas, how they show up, and what they tell you to do.

For example, Mai-Kai, a surgeon, recognizes that she often holds onto the thought, "When something is important to me, I never give up. I'm relentless." As a result, she doesn't measure how much or how little she works; she keeps attending administrative and clinical meetings, conducting research projects, performing surgeries, mentoring medical interns, and attending charity events with no regard for how long these tasks take or what they keep her from doing. When considering her health, Mai-Kai forces herself to run every day for 60 minutes, even when feeling sick, tired, or in pain, because she gets hooked on the notion of "no pain, no gain."

Now, what if I were to tell Mai-Kai to let go of these thoughts and to drop her standards? Surely she would dislike the cliché of "letting things go" because, without a doubt, all those rules have been beneficial to Mai-Kai in her career. Why should she change her actions?

Here is why: each one of us is already wired to thrive, succeed, and excel. We don't need to suffer in the process! It's that drive that is responsible for many amazing things in our world, such as the invention of writing, planes, electricity, aqueducts, medical devices, cars, digital devices, and so much more. Because of these inventions, we have been able to expand our life expectancy, cure complex medical diseases, decrease the mortality of some fatal conditions, and consider the option of living on another planet. Isn't that amazing?

At the beginning of this book I promised that I wouldn't tell you to drop your standards, do things carelessly, or do mediocre things. In fact, I think doing so can make any person feel very alienated, especially when they deeply care about stuff.

But what I can tell you is that living a life without checking what you're pursuing, why you're doing it, and how you're doing it will set you up for disappointment. Without checking your fear-based habits, you are basically always welcoming in feelings of never being enough, always being behind, or never being as good as others.

The key is *not* to drop those standards or forever let go of ruling-thoughts. The key is to get things done in a high-quality manner without wrestling with the distress, anxiety, and stress of holding strictly and rigidly to those ruling-thoughts.

The key is to learn research-based skills to live the life you want to live, do things your way, and be yourself, without the extra stuff that makes it hard to enjoy your accomplishments. You can care about your career *and* have a thriving marriage. You can spend hours on your hobby *and* attend your children's events. You can aim for straight As *and* spend time with friends on the weekend.

11 Personal Narratives

- Situation: missing an important phone call.
  A perfectionistic mind: Sasha, why don't you pay closer attention? Are you deaf? Don't you care about that call? You're too relaxed.
- Situation: skipping a detail for a project at work.
  A perfectionistic mind: this is not good for my career; I'm not good at my job. I'm a careless person.
- Situation: forgetting a deadline
  A perfectionistic mind: how did that happen? Clearly, I'm irresponsible; I should have known better. I'm an idiot.

If we look back at our lives, we find a collection of unfortunate situations that happen to all of us. There are random events, like the sink getting clogged, not finding a clean T-shirt that fits us well, receiving a letter from the IRS about our tax returns, or dealing with an earthquake. And there are also expected ones, such as losing our pet, feeling lost, feeling like an impostor, witnessing our parents aging slowly, or facing the consequences of poor financial decisions.

Even though we give our best, life has sooooooo many messy moments. We don't know when they're coming, how intense they're going to be, or how often they will happen. Messy moments just happen. What are the messy moments you have experienced so far?

In those cluttered, cumbersome, and heavy moments, your mind naturally tries to make sense of what's happening by elaborating on the events, explaining them in detail, or coming up with an entire narrative about who you are based on those unfortunate situations. In those seconds, your mind is like a lawyer citing evidence to prove your character – not with bad intentions necessarily, just doing its job.

What are the narratives that you have about yourself? In particular, what is the story in your mind when things go south, unexpected things happen, or your expectations are not met?

To answer this question, I invite you to recall a couple of times when things were challenging or hard to handle, or you felt as if you were failing yourself or others. You don't have to recall perfect examples, just

DOI: 10.4324/9781003083153-14

some moments that will help reveal some of your stories. As you do so, ask yourself these questions:

- What did I think of myself in those situations?
- How did I judge myself in those moments?
- How did I treat myself?
- What did I tell myself?
- What did I do in those moments?

Did you relate to yourself with caring, gentleness, and compassion? Or were you harsh, ultra-critical, and unforgiving with yourself? What narrative came up for you?

The truth is that when I do exercises like this with my clients, I often hear them saying things like, "I'm stupid. I'm too disorganized. I'm selfish, critical, and arrogant."

Is there a common theme running through your responses that reflects who you believe you are as a person? Are there themes of being a loser? Being defective, unworthy, unlovable, a mess, or anything else along those lines? If you identified a couple of themes, make a mental note of the ones that hurt the most – the ones that may be more present for you and that you'll need to keep an eye on.

Why would your mind generate self-critical and terrible stories about yourself? Turns out that, strange as it sounds, your mind is simply doing its job, once again. Your mind's task is to make sense of situations, so it sometimes comes up with all types of content, including a story about yourself that, though it may seem harsh, is one way of narrating what's happening in our internal and external worlds.

Our minds cannot go one day without trying to make sense of what's happening within ourselves and around us. Can you possibly imagine moving through the day without your mind narrating anything? That might sound good, but it's impossible. If you think about the evolution of the human mind, the cavewoman and caveman survived because they compared themselves to others to avoid getting rejected, killed, or left alone to survive in awful physical environments.

So, ultimately, our minds need to come up with narratives, including harsh ones, to shield us from anything that could conceivably hurt us.

Stories That Keep Us Stuck

Your personal stories about who you are may have shifted in form over time, varying from harsh, critical, and unkind to nice, upbeat, and positive. But having go-getting tendencies makes you more vulnerable to getting stuck in those narratives that are negative. Have you noticed how those personal stories could also be driving your behaviors without you being fully aware of it?

Let's consider Ameer for a moment: Ameer is afraid of being a loser, so he writes lists of positive affirmations, such as, *I'm kind. I'm a hardworking human being. I'm loving. I'm nice to others.* Other times, he lists memories of times he received positive feedback from others and tries to hold on to them. And still other times, when his mind is being critical, he argues with it and lists all the things he's doing properly in those moments.

When Ameer performs well at work, he feels great about himself – until his performance drops. He does his best to fully believe the good narratives about himself, and sometimes he feels relief from the negative ones. But it's only a matter of time until his mind comes back to the personal attacks, and he's trapped again into fighting them – and feeling crushed by them. It's like a never-ending war in his mind about his true character.

Our personal narratives are difficult because if we don't pay attention to them, we hold them as the absolute Truth, with a capital "T." We're influenced by them and go along with whatever they tell us to do. That's tricky business!

For now, it's very important that you are aware of any of these stories showing up – what starts them, what triggers them, and what behavioral patterns come with them. And instead of proving them wrong, just don't do anything; watch them without engaging with them.

As hard as it may seem, unpacking these stories is a key process toward building awareness and uncovering the influence of the narratives on your life. Over time, and as you continue reading this book, you will learn different ways to handle them instead of letting them dominate, stress, and fatigue you.

Section III

Harnessing the Power of High-Achieving and Perfectionistic Actions

While my friend and I were listening to the song "Policy of Truth" by Depeche Mode and chatting about this manuscript, he said, "I think that perfectionism is inherently wrong and pervasive."

I paused, looked at him, had a sip of my beer, and shared my view on it: like most things, perfectionism is not an either-or attribute. In fact, high-achieving actions can be described as a continuum of purposeful behaviors that are done with the goal of doing the things you care about perfectly. And if you look at your life, perfectionistic actions move back and forth along that continuum and show up in some areas of your like more than others.

Perfectionism – as you read in Section II, Unpacking Your Personal History – is also not just a single thing but a collection of private and public behaviors that are driven by other variables such as: struggling with the possibility of mistakes, fears of being a failure, negative personal narratives, rules about how you should behave, feel, and think about yourself and a situation, and a natural capacity to experience fears, worries, and anxieties.

Although fear, negative self-narratives, go-getting behaviors, high-achieving actions, and perfectionism are not new, and there are thousands of resources on them, they're usually framed as the enemies that you have to fight against and get rid of.

In all honesty, how has this approach worked for you? How many books have you read about these topics that had this tone? How many conversations have you had about getting rid of those high-achieving actions? How many long-lasting changes have you made based on all those messages that see perfectionism as the enemy within?

I have heard hundreds of stories of how approaching high-achieving actions as the enemy has actually kept people stuck, isolated, and struggling – not knowing how to be themselves, doing what they're the best at, and pursuing what's important to them. Some people had some form of success letting their standards go for a couple of times, until they were back to doing things as they usually did.

The truth is that the narrative of attacking perfectionistic actions and being told to just "let them go" hasn't worked for many people; it's not

DOI: 10.4324/9781003083153-15

just you. This is because we're looking at things in a dichotomous way – as either good or bad, positive or negative, angel or demon.

"Harnessing the power of perfectionism" is how I intentionally choose to highlight my view of perfectionism – not as evil, not as an angel, but more as a strong internal sense of caring that needs to be nurtured, cultivated, and coached.

The conversation with my friend ended with us listening to the song "Never Let Me Down Again." I took another sip of my beer and gave him a warm smile.

So, please, grab your favorite drink, find your favorite spot to read, and dive into these next pages.

12 The Future of Caring Behaviors

We all learn to care about something in our lives. When we care about something, we also learn to experience worry, fear, and nerves, all together. But, when you're sensitive to high-achieving actions, you also learn to be afraid of making mistakes, dropping things, and doing things wrong. You learn to be tough on yourself, negatively judge your actions, and hold onto narratives about who you are that are colored by your imperfections.

It's like the more you care about something, the more vulnerable you are to your stories, personal narratives, anxieties, and fears of messing up. It's like your deepest wishes for doing what you care about and your fears of doing it wrong grow together, never apart.

In an interview I did with a writer on my podcast, *Playing-It-Safe*, I was casually asking about fear-based responses. Next thing I knew, my guest was telling me about her collection of fears about not raising her kids properly, not feeding them well, doing things that may send them to therapy for the rest of their lives, getting mad so often at the disorder they create in the house, and so on.

Here is what struck me in that moment: In front of me was a person who didn't know how much motherhood meant to her until she decided to have children. When she became a mother, a strong, deep sense of caring emerged, and, there she was, full of love, dedication, and eagerness to show up for her kids. But she was also full of fear that she would make parenting mistakes (you can listen to episode 24 on the website www.playingitsafe.zone).

Think about it: there is the stuff you don't pay attention to that you couldn't care less how it works, looks, or turns out. Other things you care about, but only to a certain point. And then there are the things you care deeply about; these are the things you cannot go to sleep without thinking about.

It's quite likely that, throughout your life, the degree to which you've cared about things has shifted, changed, and varied. You may wonder, why is this important? Because the future of doing all the things you care about means checking in with yourself about which side of the continuum you are on at different times in your life.

As we touched upon in the beginning of this section, your deeply caring behaviors, your fear of making mistakes, your narratives about not

DOI: 10.4324/9781003083153-16

being good enough, and your high-achieving actions come as part of a continuum that shifts, morphs, and evolves in many directions, and in many areas of your life, at different speeds and in different ratios and shapes.

Your high-achievement-driven actions are not the enemies, but rather actions that can be nurtured, cultivated, and fostered into personal growth.

Your perfectionistic urges are natural occurrences that happen when you care deeply about something. But rather than being taken as rules, they should be treated as guideposts to help you live a meaningful life.

Besides, all the things that your brain has learned to care about? They're not going away anytime soon, or ever. So, instead of fighting against these things, the key is to learn to live with them, sit with them, make room for them – without letting them sink you.

Your caring behaviors will shift. And as you will learn, these shifts don't define you, but rather are moving parts that represent what you care about.

13 What Are Your Precious Values?

- Imagine for a moment that you live your purpose from the moment you open your eyes in the morning to the moment you fall asleep at night.
- Imagine for a moment that you create and live a life that is fulfilling, meaningful, and purposeful across the board.
- Imagine for a moment that you feel fulfilled by, satisfied with, and excited about your life, even when things get rocky, frustrating, or disappointing.
- Imagine for a moment that you say and do the things that are important to you without wrestling with worry, dealing with stress, or struggling with exhaustion.
- Imagine for a moment that you are who you want to be, stand up for what's important to you, and relate to the world in a way that matters to you.
- Imagine for a moment that you gain a sense of vitality, joy, and meaning from doing what's important to you.

Just for the record, I'm not trying to emulate John Lennon's song "Imagine"; this is my own version of what your future could look like. Wouldn't that be amazing?

Wouldn't it be amazing if, one year from now, you could see that you were doing the things that matter the most to you without sacrificing your well-being? Without dwelling on self-criticism and hurting your relationships?

Wouldn't it be amazing if you learned to nurture your drive for high achievement but could lose the sleepless nights, hours of regret, and days of blaming yourself when things go wrong?

If you're clear on what's important to you, that's great! This chapter might be a refresher for you – but promise me that you won't skip it. Keep your eyes open to see what comes to you as you read through it; you may be surprised by what you find (Hint: values are not feelings or goals).

Most of us barely take the time to wonder how we're living our lives, to think about the things that engage, revitalize, and fulfill us, on a regular day; we just keep doing what we're supposed to be doing. Some

DOI: 10.4324/9781003083153-17

people go along with what their families, religion, or political systems tell them about the meaning of life. We all know how to worry and speculate about, and analyze, our lives for hours while sitting next to a glass of good scotch, but none of that will lead us to discover what's important to us. So this chapter is about figuring out your values, your true treasures, your gems.

Ask anyone their opinions on an issue like politics, the environment, social justice, religion, or ethics, and you will hear about what "ought to be" and how things "should be." Ask your friends about their favorite books, movies, or music, and you will likely get powerful responses explaining what they appreciate in each one and how it relates to them. Ask a teenager to flip through the hundreds of photos on their mobile phone and share the ones that are special to them, and you will hear about moments from their life that capture what's important to them. Every single person on earth wants to live with meaning, purpose, and intention.

Within ACT, we think of values in a very unique way. We look at them through the lens of some key questions: what kind of life do you want to live? What sort of person do you want to be? What kind of relative do you want to be? Are you being the friend you want to be? Are you treating yourself the way you really, truly, deep in your heart want to be treated? Very different, right?

It doesn't matter where you come from, where you think you're going, or what you are doing these days. Your values are like a compass that should give you clear direction on which way to go. And you're not too late or too early to figure out your true north.

When discussing what's deep down important to my clients and introducing how ACT thinks of values, I usually hear a number of questions. My responses to these questions are as follows.

Take a careful look at them so we can be on the same page as you move forward with living your life with purpose, getting better at managing those fears of making mistakes and not being good enough, and addressing those urges to do things perfectly.

How Do Values Relate to Feelings?

When we're living our values, there is a large range of emotions that comes our way – from the most comfortable ones to the most stressful ones and everything in between. But, overall, there is a strong sense of vitality, engagement, and meaning that we experience when we do the things that matter most to us.

The challenge is that, at times, people confuse a feeling with a value – but feelings are just feelings. Our feelings, our emotions, are more like waves on the ocean; they come and go. Living your values is not about feeling good all the time. In fact, doing what matters comes with uncomfortable feelings at times.

When writing this book, I felt all types of emotions – from excitement, joy, and curiosity to fatigue, stress, fear, and others. Many days when I sat down to write, I had all those feelings in the background as uninvited guests doing their own thing; but, I was super-clear about why I was writing these pages. Every time I made the choice to sit with all the feelings that showed up and kept writing, that choice gave me a unique sense of vitality. It's like every time I finished my writing session, I knew deep in my heart that I was doing what mattered. I was clear about my commitment to this project and what it meant to me.

If our values were merely emotions, they would die as soon as the emotions that came with them ended. Our feelings, all of them, arise and disappear, only to arise and disappear again. Values, on the other hand, are constant choices we make, regardless of what we feel.

Mini-Tip

Having one feeling versus another does not mean you're living your values; you're just feeling.

What If I Value Being Happy, Peaceful, and Smiley?

Alman grew up in a house listening to comments like, "Being happy, optimistic, and positive are good attributes; you'll attract good people in your life, and life is better if you walk with a smile on your face."

If your mind says that the outcome you want in life is to feel happy, bubbly, and peaceful at all times, I totally get it; it's understandable because those emotions are enjoyable and can be contagious to others. But I have to break the news to you: you don't have control over what you feel; neither do I. For a moment, don't listen to me and instead do a mini-exercise: tell yourself to be excited in this moment and do your best to feel excited.

When I tell myself to feel one way or another, I may be able to mimic the facial expression of that particular emotion, but emotions cannot be induced in that way. Different events and circumstances can trigger happy feelings, but they vanish as soon as circumstances change.

Sometimes our desire to be happy is masking our hurts; behind those hurts is the stuff we care about.

Mini-Tip

So, if your mind insists on making your life about being happy, I would invite you to ask yourself: what happens if I don't feel happy? What's hard about having that feeling or experience? What important thing is that feeling or experience showing me?

Are Values the Same as the Things I Like to Do?

We all have stuff we like to do – love to do, even – and want to do more of. For instance, you may love watching your favorite TV show, drinking your favorite beer, reading your favorite stories, wearing a particular pair of shoes, and chatting with your best friends. All of those activities are nice and fun, and you may want to have a lot of those moments, but they are preferences, not values.

As fun as these activities are, they are all things that you like, prefer, and choose to do; that's great. But doing these activities doesn't necessarily mean that you're living your values.

Living your values goes beyond living your preferences. Living your values is about checking what your actions are in service of.

Mini-Tip

When doing any of your favorite activities, you may want to ask yourself: what's this activity in service of?

What If One of My Values Is "Wanting to Be Respected by Others"?

It's very understandable; we all want to be respected, appreciated, and seen by others. But, and this is a big "but," as much as we want to experience all these things from others, we just don't have control over others' reactions to, behavior toward, or feelings about us. We cannot make people respect us, love us, or see us. We don't have a device that can program how others will respond to us; and often, the more that we try to control others' behaviors toward us, the less likely it is they will do so. Since it's out of our control how others feel, behave, and think about us, those cannot be your values!

But, if you do what's in your control and behave with respect, appreciate others, and do your best to understand them, then it's possible that you will feel respected, appreciated, and seen in return.

Mini-Tip

When exploring your values, if your mind demands that you focus on getting a particular behavior or action from others, ask yourself: what matters so much to me about that response from others? What is the hurt showing me that I care about?

Are Values the Same as Goals?

This is a very popular question. I wish I got a delicious cup of coffee every time I answered it! Joking aside, here is my response: goals are specific stepping-stones and actions that move you in the direction of your values and that, once completed, are checked off the list. But your values are the "why" behind what you do.

For instance, if your aim is to get married, that's a goal. Once you get married, that goal is achieved. But if you want to create a long-lasting relationship with your partner, you'll need to ask yourself questions like: what type of partner do I want to be? What are the qualities I want to bring to the relationship? What's important to me about committing to another person? You may figure out that protecting, listening to, and being present with your partner are your values and the qualities for you to bring to the relationship.

Since we're always working towards our values, within ACT we think of values as verbs because they involve ongoing, constant, and endless actions!

Mini-Tip

When thinking about your values, make sure to distinguish between desired outcomes – goals – that you want to achieve, which are things that could be crossed off a to-do list, and the qualities you want to embrace in that particular area of your life.

What about important rules?

This is another popular question I hear from high achievers: what if my values include "to always give my best; to always do things with caring; to always try hard; to always do things the right way"?

In Chapter 10, Mental Rubrics, you read about different types of ruling-thoughts about how you should behave, what success is, how you should this or that. And of course, your mind will associate all of those ruling-thoughts with values. Here is the deal: ruling-thoughts tell you the right and wrong way of doing things, but values show you the quality you want to bring to your action. So, "you shouldn't leave a restaurant without paying for your meal" is a rule. It tells you how you should behave and what you shouldn't do. But the value underneath that rule is caring, consideration, and respect for the owners of the restaurant.

Of course, your mind can protest and say, "but that rule is super-important to me." So, suppose that you decided to do groceries for your elderly neighbor because she cannot leave her apartment much these days. You can do grocery shopping for her because you're in touch with your value: being kind. But what if you do grocery shopping for your neighbor because you're consumed with the rule, "It's the right thing to do; I always have to be kind"? Which one of these two possibilities is more revitalizing? To do things for pressure or to do things as a personal choice?

Mini-Tip

Thinking of your personal values as rules can be extremely restrictive, feel like an obligation, and a become a burden for you. Choosing your values gives you the freedom to put them into action in many different ways. So, keep in mind this important difference between rules and values.

Living your values is something you're always working toward – figuring out what matters to you and taking all the necessary steps to be who you want to be. The more steps you take toward becoming that person, the better it gets. Your values are your precious gems that direct your choices and give you direction; and, amid conflictive situations, unexpected difficulties, or contradicting choices, they will show you how to navigate those moments without losing yourself (you can listen to episode 23 for an overview on values on the website www.playingitsafe.zone).

14 Does It Really Matter?

Life is both amazing and hard. But when you're guided by your precious values in everything you do, and you keep doing what matters to you, you experience a sense of vitality, engagement, and meaningfulness that is priceless. Think for a moment of my good friend Sean.

Sean grew up in a small suburban town, working class, and was raised by his single mother because, when he was about six years old, his father abandoned them. Sean grew up listening to U2, enjoying sports, and having low-key hangouts with friends. While Sean and his mom weren't financially deprived, his mom worked really hard to provide for both of them; with a single-income female breadwinner, it wasn't easy at times. Sean's mom graciously provided the basics for him, and while he knew that he didn't have as much as some other classmates, he felt grateful for his mother's hard work and knew that he needed to work hard to avoid future struggles.

As he grew up, he graduated from high school and, driven by his desire for a secure future, pursued a degree in business, which he successfully completed. Then, focused again on his financial security, he chased a master of business administration degree, which he also completed.

By the time he graduated, he was offered a job in a large corporation, which he quickly accepted and was eager to start. Sean's family was very proud of him, and his mom put together a special gathering to celebrate his accomplishments. Sean had the enthusiasm and energy of a recently graduated student; he was ready to be financially independent, to conquer and work as hard as needed to succeed in the financial world. He worked in the finance department of a large health organization for more than 15 years, was able to buy an apartment in a large city, paid the mortgage on his mom's house, took annual vacations to different countries, and started a retirement account. On paper, Sean had a good life, a perfect life.

But every year that passed, Sean doubted himself more; he doubted what he was doing, questioned his happiness, and queried his success. He couldn't make sense of what was wrong, given all his career accomplishments, success, and achievements. He couldn't make sense of how every day he dragged his feet to the office and how he no longer felt excited about work; his friends criticized him for not appreciating what he had accomplished so far. Sean finished every day with a strong sense of emptiness, disconnection, and despair. He started managing those feelings by going out to the local bar, first on Wednesdays and weekends; then, every other day and weekends.

Sean became aware of how much he was drinking and his now perpetual struggle with his career and decided to take a week off. That week, he didn't drink and he stayed in his apartment by himself, trying to figure out what had gone wrong and why he was no longer happy even though he had the one thing he'd dreamed about as a kid: financial security.

He wrote on a piece of paper all the things he disliked about his career; the list kept growing longer and longer. He couldn't believe how much he had been pushing himself to do things that instead of energizing him were draining his enthusiasm. Then he tried to list the things he liked about his job; this list was a bit shorter. Next, he looked at other things he spent time on: playing and watching sports, gathering with friends and family, and volunteering at the animal shelter. Sean did the same thing for each one of those activities – he wrote down what he liked about it and what he didn't.

When Sean was writing about his time at the local animal shelter, he noticed how excited he was every month to go clean cages, walk and pet animals, and prepare animals for adoption. He started remembering how every last Saturday of the month, he would make his lunch ahead of time and make sure nothing on the calendar conflicted with his volunteer time at the shelter.

As he continued to ponder about his time at the shelter, he started crying and couldn't stop. He cried alone for hours inside the walls of his apartment. He realized that rather than creating his life, life was happening to him. He felt lost, confused, and sad about the fact that what had appeared to be his main driver in life may not have been everything. Sean realized that while financial security was still important to him, his whole life didn't need to be dictated by it.

As time passed, Sean started taking classes at the local veterinary school, training as a veterinary technician, while he continued working at his firm. As tempted as he was by every possibility of a raise or promotion within his firm, he continued taking classes at the local veterinary school. It took him five years to graduate as a veterinary technician rather than the three years it takes most people.

The day Sean left his company, his friends asked him one more time: are you sure this is what you want to do? You know these opportunities don't come every single day, and you already have 18 years invested in this career. Sean listened to each one of his friends and recalled conversations with his mom about it too. He was afraid – scared of making this shift – and had big doubts about what was coming next and what it would look like. But he knew that he couldn't hide any longer behind the business of work and the big checks he received monthly.

The things that matter deeply to us, our answers to the questions of why we're here and what our life's about, can guide us every single day – even when things get rocky, we feel lost, or awful things happen to us.

15 Important Questions, Important Answers

Deep down inside, what do you really want your life to be about?

It's easy for our minds to quickly answer that question, and yet, let's remember that our minds also carry with them countless pieces of input about how we should be living our lives in their own. All those quick responses to how you want to live your life can be truthful, but it's better to check once again. Think about all those areas in your life in which you push yourself hard, go beyond what's expected, and strive to give your best at all times for this reflection. What do you really want your life to be about in those areas?

Instead of quickly answering this question or rushing to a decision, I invite you to give yourself some time to reflect and really tap into your heart's deepest desires for how you want to live your life and how you want to relate to yourself, others, and the world.

The exercise that follows is based on the work of different psychologists (Blacklege & Ciarocchi, 2006) and focuses on six different areas of life: (1) romantic relationships, (2) parenting, (3) friendships, (4) work and career, (5) personal growth, and (6) family relationships.

I don't mean to be like your grandmother here, but on behalf of the life you want to build, please make sure to do this exercise. Put on your favorite background music, minimize distractions, find a comfortable and quiet place, and answer each one of the questions that follow about your values in these areas of our life.

(1) Romantic relationships:

What kind of partner do you want to be to your significant other?
How do you want to show up for your relationship?
How would you treat others if you were behaving as the partner you want to be?

(2) Parenting:

What's important to you in parenting your kids?
How would you like to be remembered by your kids?
What are the qualities that are deeply important for you as a parent?

DOI: 10.4324/9781003083153-19

(3) Friendships:

How do you want to show up for your friends?
What matters to you in how you approach your friendships?
How would you like to treat your friends when being the friend you want to be?

(4) Family relationships:

What is most important to you about your relationships with your parents and siblings?

(5) Personal growth:

What's important to you when you think about your physical, mental, and emotional lives?
What's important to you in your spiritual or religious life?
How do you want to show up for others in your community?
How do you want to unwind, relax, or reset?

(6) Work and career:

What are the personal qualities you want to bring to your work or studies?
How do you want to behave with others while at work or school?

The questions about what's important to you in your relationships – all types of them – are about how you want to behave, not how others should behave or how you would like them to relate to you. You only have control over your behaviors (You can find a list of values on the page "ACT for Perfectionism and High-Achieving Actions" on my personal website: https://www.thisisdoctorz.com/act-for-perfectionism-and-high-achieving-behaviors/).

Think back on your answers and ask yourself:

- Which of these values am I actively living right now?
- Which of these values do I need to work on?

Having clarity on how you're living your life never gets old, because every time you pause and check what's going on in your day-to-day life gives you an opportunity to choose in which direction to move, what to do more, what to do less, what to start, or what to stop doing.

And trust me, when you choose to live your values day by day, life becomes much more satisfying, invigorating, and refreshing than it has ever been before. A values-based life is not like a classic Hollywood movie with a happy ending (there's nothing wrong with liking these movies, of course). A values-based life is not a pain-free, struggle-free, or hassle-free one, but choosing when the pain, struggle, and hassle are worth the trouble makes a huuuuuuuuuuuge difference.

16 One Year From Now

Imagine that a year from now you look back and see that you have been taking steps in different areas of your life, one by one, toward living your values, without getting consumed with making perfect decisions, feeling guilty if you're not doing more, or ensuring that every single thing you do is an accurate representation of your character.

Imagine that a year from now you accomplish the tasks you care about with carefulness and dedication, without the stress that comes from triple-guessing yourself, working yourself to exhaustion, or criticizing yourself for not doing things perfectly.

Imagine that a year from now you take care of the ones you love, say what you really think, and do what's important to you without sacrificing your well-being, placating, or wrestling with stories of not being good enough.

Wouldn't that be neat?

Within ACT, we're very invested in translating your personal values into specific and concrete actions you can take, day by day. It doesn't matter the size of the step you take; what's important is why you do it, how you do it, and how you show up for it.

If you want to live a values-based life, you cannot live your values by taking random steps in any direction; your steps must be committed, intentional, and purposeful. It's like, if I wanted to travel to Bolivia, I wouldn't make it there if I took a plane to Japan, right? Living a purposeful life is the same, so you better pay attention to which way you're going.

Here is what you need to do to live congruently with your values: please go ahead, make a mark on this page, put this book down, grab some sheets of paper and a pen, and then come back to this page. I mean it.

Once you have a paper and a pen, write at the top of each page a brief description of your values for each of the six areas we discussed in Chapter 15, Important Questions, Important Answers: (1) romantic relationships, (2) parenting, (3) friendships, (4) career/education, (5) personal growth, and (6) family relationships.

Then, for each value, write down specific goals, actions, and steps you want to take. If you're living your values in some of the areas already,

DOI: 10.4324/9781003083153-20

then focus on the ones you want to improve. To be clear about your goals, you answer these questions:

- What specific, concrete actions can I take?
- When would I take these actions?
- With whom would I take these steps?

Some of the actions might be things you can do immediately; some may be short-term steps and others long-term. It's likely some of the steps will be small, others medium, and still others large.

Remember Sean, from Chapter 14? He chose "being protective of animals' lives" as a value in the area of career/education, so he decided to study to be a veterinary technician (a long-term goal), to continue volunteering once a month at the animal shelter for the next 12 months (an immediate goal), to subscribe to two magazines about animal rights (an immediate goal), to prepare a budget for his education (a short-term goal), and to research what's needed to run a clinic or sanctuary for animals (a short-term goal).

I'm not suggesting that you write these things down to bother you or nag you. I'm asking you to jot things down more with the intention of guiding you in building the habit of doing the things that are truly important to you and keeping yourself on track when doing so – even beyond this book.

You see, living your values means living them with your feet, hands, and mouth, and you can only do that when you make the time to do so, commit to doing it, and then do it.

Moving forward, I urge you to create some form of weekly tracking for how you're living your values; any system that you like should work. For instance, in one corner of the whiteboard in my office, I have written down the three areas – relationships, career, personal growth – that I focus on; next to each one of those areas there is a straight line. Each line represents a continuum: on one end, I'm closely living that value, and on the other, I'm far from living it. Every week, I make an "x" in each one of those lines based on how I have been acting on my values the week before. No one knows what it represents; it's a very personal way of keeping myself in check and, believe me, it makes a difference.

No matter what tracking system you use to live your values, try to make it visible, so you can see yourself building momentum toward the things that, deep inside, matter most to you.

Picture for a moment how it would be if, instead of checking off tasks from your to-do list because that's what you need to do that day, you checked off goals, actions, and steps toward your precious values? Or imagine how it would it be if, instead of choosing to do things with the only purpose of minimizing the fear of being a failure, the possibility of things going wrong, or disappointing others, you choose to do those things because they move you towards living your values. Quite different, right?

And just to clarify, I'm not saying that you shouldn't do all the chores that need taking care of – cooking, grocery shopping, cleaning, and so on. I'm just saying that life is about more than getting these things done.

Living your values is more like having infinite time horizons; there is no end or finish line, and there is no such thing as living your values perfectly. There is choosing to live with purpose, meaning, and fulfillment every moment you're alive.

"Doing Things Right" Is the Right Thing to Do, at Times

When you're doing things that matter to you, you will, of course, encounter all types of blocks. Many obstacles and events will get in your way – health problems, family gatherings, feelings of fatigue, work responsibilities, doubtful thoughts, and more. It's no one's fault; it's just the nature of life.

Your mind may protest, throw tantrums, and demand that you do things the old way, that you do them faster, perfectly, or better, and that you do more and more. This is a super-tricky collection of thoughts that, if they go unchecked, can easily take you on detours away from your values.

When working on this manuscript, I recalled the many conversations I'd had over the years with clients and friends about perfectionistic actions, fears of failing, self-criticism, and the push to work relentlessly. I studied many research articles. I went back to old jotted notes about moments in which I felt stuck in my work with clients. And, of course, I chatted with some of my close friends and acquaintances about these topics.

One of the people I spoke to told me, "Patricia, I have no desire to lessen my attention to detail or my desire for perfection; I see these things as attributes. . . . I'm sure most people I work with see them [attention to detail and perfectionistic behaviors] as attributes, and anything less is settling for subpar quality."

Former clients of mine said:

> "Why should I do less than what I'm capable of?"
> "Why should I do mediocre work?"
> "Why should I stop giving my best?"

I could write a separate book about the thousands of arguments my clients have shared with me about why it doesn't make sense to let go of avoiding mistakes, having high standards, and staying thirsty for perfection when they're doing the things they care about. If that book were to be published, I would suggest the title *One Hundred and One Ways to Do Things Perfectly*.

One thing is very clear to me: high-achieving behaviors are resistant to change. End of story!

Think about it: after so many years of doing things in a particular way, thinking about things in a particular way, and feeling about things in a particular way, of course these old ways of doing, thinking, and feeling have become second nature. After so many years of managing your fears of failing by using a series of public and private behaviors that help you feel good temporarily but reinforce that habit of doing more and more, shouldn't you expect to feel the pull to repeat the same actions again and again – even if you're ready to make a change and try something new?

Getting stuck between old and new learnings is normal because when we try something new, our brains get wild and push hard to return to what's familiar.

The ways in which those resistant-to-change thoughts (e.g., *it doesn't make sense to let go of high-achieving behaviors*) can show up are countless. Since there are no limits to what our minds can come up with, who knows how many more variations on those thoughts will appear in your mind over the course of your lifetime and how many more I'll hear over the course of mine?

Now, check for yourself: How many times have you tried to let go of pushing yourself beyond limits when doing something you cared about, only to realize that your efforts lasted just a couple of days?

I cannot answer for you, but I bet that you've done your best many, many times to shake those old high-achieving behaviors, and yet, without even realizing it, you returned to relying on those same old standards.

Your mind will give you numerous reasons why doing things exactly right is the right thing to do. On top of that, when you care deeply about something, when something truly matters to you, it doesn't make sense to drop the ball. Why should you?

The reality is that our minds are super talented at coming up with reasons to do the same old, same old. To this end, your mind will bring up familiar narratives: *what if I fail trying to do something different? What if nothing works in the end? What if I end up with the same stress that I had before and worse? What if my family is negatively affected by my irresponsible actions as I'm trying to do something more balanced?* And on and on.

If you engage with, entertain, or even argue with these narratives, you could easily spend hours debating yourself rather than taking new steps.

When your mind comes up with all these reasons, do your best to step back and look at how things will work for you if you keep doing what you have been doing. What will happen to your life if you keep holding yourself responsible for others' well-being beyond your own capacities and at all times? What will happen if you keep avoiding starting things until you're sure you have collected all the necessary information? What happens when you relentlessly pursue the things you care about without checking how things are going in other areas of your life?

I'm sure that if you have read this book up to this chapter, you have tried many things to deal with your fears of failing, being an impostor, and not doing things right all the time. How did they work?

You see, I'm not here to tell you that high-achieving behaviors are demons, because as you have heard me saying before, wanting to do things to high standards, striving to do your best, and pursuing what you care about with close attention to detail are not the problems. The problem is how you go about doing the things that are important to you, how these actions affect your life, and how revitalizing (or not) they are for you.

That's why it is super important for you to keep in mind that doing things right is the right thing to do, at times. And, sometimes, letting things go can also be the right thing to do. But how do you make that distinction?

18 What Game Are You Playing?

In the movie *Stranger Than Fiction*, Will Ferrell plays a character named Harold Crick, an impeccable IRS agent who one day starts hearing the story of his life narrated inside his mind. Understandably, he is confused and scared. As Crick tries to understand what's happening to him, he realizes he needs to figure out if the story being written about him is a comedy or a tragedy, so he can prepare himself.

In one of my favorite scenes, Crick walks into the bakery he's auditing; looks at the owner, a woman he has a crush on, and feels his heart immediately start sinking. He's unable to get out a full sentence and instead mumbles a couple of words. In response, she looks at him, with big, open eyes, and angrily asks, "What do you want, Tax Man?"

Crick slowly moves his hands to his pocket, grabs a little notepad, and, using one of the pens from his collection of matching pens, jots down:

Tragedy X
Comedy 0

In this way, Crick keeps track of each situation that arises as his day unfolds. I won't spoil the movie for you, but I highly recommend it if you like watching stories with a touch of humor, connection, struggle, and love.

So, if you reflect back on all the times you pushed yourself to do things right, worked relentlessly, moved from one project onto the next, set new larger, better, and bigger goals for yourself, and didn't let anyone over because your house wasn't perfectly clean, what kind of life story do you think you were living?

- A story in which you've been relentlessly trying to do things correctly all the time without checking how it's working?

    or...

- One in which you've been working toward living a fulfilling, rich, and purposeful life, doing the things you care about to the best of your abilities without hurting your health, well-being, or relationships?

DOI: 10.4324/9781003083153-22

What would you say?

Living the story of "doing things perfectly all the time" has many pros: you accomplish, achieve, and feel a high when you've gotten things with high quality. You get things done, you look in the way you want to look, you say the right things, you excel in what you do, you master the nitty-gritty details of a task, you make the optimal decision in any given situation, and you take good care of others. Who would want to stop all that?

But – and this is a big "but" – living your life this way can also lead to problems, because if something goes wrong or doesn't go as you expected it to, it's like opening the door to a tornado of harsh self-criticism, self-doubt, and hours of wrestling in your head. You may achieve your goals, but you also may be dealing with ripple effects: actions in other areas of your life being postponed, mental fatigue, intense distress in your body as your adrenaline goes up and down, negative effects on your relationships with others due to all the time spent reaching for your goals.

What if, instead of "doing things perfectly all the time," your life story becomes one about reaching for a fulfilling life by doing, to high standards, the things you care deeply about, paying attention to details, and generating awesome quality without dealing with high levels of anxiety, harsh criticism when things go wrong, or people in your life telling you that they're feeling ignored?

This second option is called *playing the workability game*. When you play the workability game, you:

- Figure out a way to make things happen with excellence, high standards, and tons of caring while getting a good night's sleep, evenings out with the people you care about, and regular physical activity.
- Manage all those worries about making mistakes or being seen as an impostor without wrestling with, battling, or spending unnecessary time on those thoughts.
- Deal with all the noise that shows up in your mind in a way that is not paralyzing, overwhelming, or annoying.
- Build the resiliency, flexibility, and adaptability needed to deal with the unpredictable and uncertain world we live in.
- Create habits to make the most of your time, focus on what you care about, and effectively handle all the decisions you need to make to pursue your goals.
- Ditch other people's definitions of success, accomplishment, and well-being to pursue your own.
- Bring all your expertise, knowledge, and caring to what you do without struggling with the negative effects on your well-being, health, and personal growth.
- Develop a new mindset to do the things you care deeply about well, without negatively affecting other areas of your life in the long run.

What do you say?

Section IV

The Workability Game

Welcome to one of my favorite sections of this book!

I truly hope that, by now, you have noticed that a major theme in this book is to deconstruct black-and-white views of high-achieving actions and perfectionistic behaviors and to get out of dichotomous narratives involving either-or actions, angels and demons, or sweet and sour when thinking about them.

By now you have learned that behind everything you strive to do well, there is something that is important to you. You want to do things right because you care (see Section I). You have learned how your perfectionistic and high-achieving behaviors started and what maintains them (see Section II). You have learned how acceptance and commitment skills invite you to build the life you want to live and how you can take steps toward living your precious values (see Section III). And in the previous chapter, I introduced you to the workability game.

You have heard me say in different ways that your high-achieving and perfection-driven actions are not the enemies, but rather are drivers that can be nurtured, coached, and fostered to lead to your personal growth.

In this section, I'm really excited to introduce you to different skills to help you make the best of all those go-getting, self-starting, and perfectionistic actions in a fun, doable, and livable way. I call this new way the workability game!

In the chapters ahead, you're going to learn the key principles to playing the workability game, so as you live a fulfilling life, you can mine all those high-achieving and perfectionistic actions for the gold buried within them – without the yucky stuff that normally comes with these actions.

DOI: 10.4324/9781003083153-23

19 Learning About It

Workability is one of my favorite themes in ACT! I love it so much that I considered having it tattooed on me. Just kidding, although it's not a bad idea because breathing and living workability have been incredibly refreshing, invigorating, and engaging for my life.

To be honest, putting workability into action gave me the tools I needed to handle every moment of the day in a way that felt truer to who I want to be, including when I'm feeling super cranky. So I encourage you to take this chapter to heart, make it yours, and, more important, do something with it!

When playing the workability game, there are four principles to consider:

1. The function of thinking, or the dynamic mind
2. The true essence of workability
3. The choices you make
4. The richness of your precious values

Let's dive into each one of these.

1. The Dynamic Nature of Your Mind

Let's do a mini-exercise: grab a timer, set it for two minutes, close this book, and watch, observe, or note what your mind does. If you find yourself judging your thoughts or experiencing a pull to respond to them, do your best to simply watch them and let them go.

How was this exercise for you? Did your mind come up with any thoughts about your day? The movie you want to watch? Your dinner? An awful image about your past? A romantic date you had? Worries about money? A random image of a beer? Did you have a lot of pictures or words coming into your mind?

You see, the reality is that our minds will never stop telling us "Blah blah blah," or as my aunt says in Spanish, "Cha cha cha."

Your mind, just like mine, has a life of its own, doesn't take breaks, doesn't take holidays, is in motion 24/7; it doesn't stop relating and relating, connecting and connecting, and generating thousands and

DOI: 10.4324/9781003083153-24

thousands of bits of content – always, anywhere. No matter our gender, age, ethnic background, political orientation, religious beliefs, or musical tastes, our minds are on blah-blah-blah mode all the time.

Imagine for a moment what would happen if you accepted all of your thoughts as true, important, or as evidence that something is wrong with you, and you addressed them as such. Imagine spending your time addressing and acting on every single thought that popped up in your mind. As one of my clients said, "It's a headache." I can tell you that, for me, it's truly a headache when I get consumed with thinking, dwelling, and mulling; before I know it, the time has flown by and I haven't done much besides staying in my head.

Do you see why it's ultra-important to acknowledge the dynamic nature of your mind without sinking with it?

Do you see why it's ultra-important to acknowledge the dynamic nature of your mind and work with it?

Do you see why it's ultra-important to look at how well your thoughts are working for you?

Let's move onto the next principle for playing the workability game!

2. The True Essence of Workability

If you watch the popular TV show *Dr. Phil*, you may have heard him say, "How does it work?" If you're not familiar with the show, check out any of the episodes, and you will hear Dr. Phil asking this question in one form or another.

Dr. Phil's question *How does it work?* and the question *How does that thought work for you?* – which is a question I might ask – may sound the same, but the way I think about it, and the way ACT understands it, makes the questions quite different from one another.

I'll explain the difference: most people, especially the ones that didn't read this book, think that "workability" is related to "things being workable" and use the terms interchangeably to mean doing what's right, accurate, rational, and true.

- Sanjay is afraid of being rejected and feels anxious when attending gatherings at work or going out with friends. He thinks, *What if they think I'm weird? What if they don't like me?* As a result, he comes up with excuses to turn down invitations, he doesn't call or text his friends to hang out, and he only attends family gatherings for 30 minutes. For Sanjay, avoiding social situations works to manage those anxious feelings and fears of being rejected.
- Sidney, a video editor, has a very packed schedule when he's working on a film. He checks his schedule at the beginning and end of every day to make sure he's keeping track of the different scenes he needs to work on. To make sure he doesn't get behind, he spends every weekend at the studio. Sidney feels stressed if he's not at the studio every Sunday morning – for him, being at the studio works to manage his stress.

- Deedee, a mother of two children, greatly values being present for her kids and teaching them proper manners. One evening, when hanging out with her neighbors, she noticed how one of her sons, Michael, barely responded to any of the questions he was asked about school, didn't use his utensils correctly, and spilled his food all over his area at the table. Deedee felt embarrassed about her son's behavior and thought, *I may be doing something wrong and raising disrespectful kids; my neighbor may think I'm incompetent and not really educating my kids.* Quickly, to manage these thoughts, Deedee started listing in her mind different times that her kids misbehaved in social gatherings and then times when they behaved properly. She tried to look for any indication that her neighbor was disappointed in her as a mother. At the end of the gathering, after dwelling in her mind most of the evening and being almost absent from conversation, Deedee felt relieved and noticed that her neighbor didn't say anything or behave in a different way toward her.

Let's go over each one of these situations: Sanjay managed his anxiety about rejection and fear of failure by avoiding social gatherings. Sidney handled his distress about being behind by overworking. Deedee managed her thoughts of being "an incompetent mother" by listing in her mind all the encounters that proved or disproved that narrative and paying extra attention to her neighbor's behavior toward her.

From the outside, looking in at these situations, you could say that each individual's response was working for them, that acting based on their thoughts was an effective strategy. But if you take another look, the actions Sanjay, Sidney, and Deedee took in response to their thoughts all involved a form of minimizing uncomfortable worries, fears, and anxieties. That's not how ACT thinks of workability. ACT always thinks of workability in regard to your values.

Let me clarify a couple of things so we can be on the same page and so you won't stop reading or make a confused face.

Within ACT, we're more invested in what works for you so you can live your values and do what's truly important to you instead of battling your mind over what's true, right, or accurate. Think about it: how often do you spend hours in your head trying to build an argument to prove a particular point to yourself or someone else? How often do you mull over, dwell on, or chew over why others don't see something the same way as you? Is it really worth your time and attention? Do these actions help you be who you want to be? Or is this another way in which you get stuck playing that "doing things right all the time" game?

I'm not saying that some facts aren't true or anything like that; I'm saying that workability in the context of the work we're doing in this book – and hopefully in your life – is all about looking at how a behavior helps you be who you want to be or takes you further away from it.

Let's delve deeper into this idea. What does it mean to check whether something is workable or not? Everything you do, whether it's inside or outside your head, public or private, is a behavior, and it can move you away from or toward the things that truly matter to you. Let's have a look at two scenarios to make sense of this key idea:

- Scenario 1. For breakfast, I make myself a delicious parfait with gluten-free oats, strawberries, yogurt, almond milk, carob, and a dash of vanilla.

    I prepare this breakfast a couple of mornings during the week.

- Scenario 2. I feel distressed, angry, and frustrated while watching the news, so I make sure to always have a large parfait with extra sugar and two bars of chocolate to manage my emotions and distract myself from them, even though this eating behavior has costs to my health later on.

Do you see the difference? The same behavior, eating a parfait, can be a move toward or away from the stuff that we care about, based on the situation, the context, or the setting we're in.

Checking the workability of your behaviors is best thought of as checking to see if you're living your life with direction, meaning, and vitality, and focusing on the results of your behaviors rather than arguing in your mind about what's right or what's wrong, what's accurate or what's not.

So checking the workability of your actions, especially the high-achieving and perfectionistic ones, is what truly gives you the power to live life as you want to live it.

The next principle of the workability game is focused on...

3. The Importance of Choosing Your Actions – All of Them

Every single day, we make a ridiculous number of choices – choices about what to eat, what to wear, who to hang out with, how to do a project, who to work with, what TV show to watch, how hard to push ourselves, what to say, and muuuuuuuuuch more. Our abilities for choosing stuff to do is usually very well developed, but playing the workability game means that you need to pay extra attention to how you respond to your private experiences, such as your thoughts, feelings, emotions, and sensations.

We have agreed by now that none of us have control over what our dynamic minds come up with, but we do have a choice about how to respond to each one of those thoughts, images, pictures, or sensations that show up. Think about it: let's say a worry thought pops up, asking, *What if people think I'm rude?* You can argue back, try to convince yourself that you're not rude, play back past scenarios to see if you behaved rudely, or criticize yourself – or you can notice that thought and decide how you want to respond to it given what's happening with you and what's important to you at that particular moment.

I'm not saying that you shouldn't reflect on some thoughts about who you are, how you behave, or how you're living your life; I'm saying that there is a time and place for everything, including personal reflections, and that – sorry for repeating myself here – you don't need to act based on every single picture, image, or thought that comes to mind. You don't need to automatically answer thinking with more thinking or respond to worries with more worries. You don't need to prolong your struggles relying on thinking strategies that make things worse for you.

And given that you're susceptible to working too hard and always giving your best no matter what, you need to pay attention to the choices you make when dealing with tricky thoughts, feelings, and sensations.

Here are the specific signs to watch out for:

a. When you experience fear-based emotions.

    It's a given that, every time you do what's important to you and you do it with all the care you believe it deserves, you will experience a shade of a fear-based emotion. Because you care deeply about things, you're more vulnerable to all those fears that you read about in the Chapter 7, Chapter 8, and Chapter 9: The Many Shades of Fear, Mistakes, Errors, Flaws, and A Special Type of Fear, respectively.

    You will feel some form of fear about being a failure, making mistakes, being an impostor, or dropping things. Sometimes these fears can feel like a gentle soaker. Other times they may be like a mild storm. And still other times, they can seem as loud as a thunderstorm. But every fear-based emotion you experience fuels you to act and demands that you think about something, say something, or do something; because of that, you have to keep an eye on them when they show up.

b. When your mind moves into criticism, harsh talk, and judgment.

    Every time your mind comes up with judgments about who you are – *You're an idiot. What's wrong with you; are you stupid? You're clearly not smart enough. Why are you so weird?* – those are thoughts to watch. It's important to remember that you have a choice as to how to handle, manage, and deal with them. You don't need to be at the mercy of these negative self-judgments.

c. When your mind gets hooked on ruling-thoughts.

    In Chapter 10, Mental Rubrics, you learned that one of the ways our minds make sense of all the stuff that comes their way is by creating ruling-thoughts. You learned that ruling-thoughts – *ought, should, must, always, either-or* – and strong preferences are very special because they can be inflexible and more resistant to change. Automatically going along with each one of them makes you a prisoner of your mind – and, consequently, a prisoner of ineffective high-achieving actions. So watch out for them!

d. When you feel urges, impulses, or desires to go back to the old ways of doing things perfectly.

> As you learn to harness the power of high-achieving behaviors without wrestling with the yucky stuff that comes with them – overthinking, ruminating, criticizing yourself – you will have urges, impulses, and desires to go back to the old ways of pushing yourself hard, giving your best indiscriminately, taking your mind too seriously, or protecting yourself relentlessly from any possibility of failure. That's natural; old behaviors fight for survival. But every time you feel that push, it usually means that there is a choice that you need to make.

To put it all together: these fear-based emotions, harsh criticisms, ruling-thoughts, and urges to go back to the old ways of doing things right and perfect, are your choice points – your opportunities to choose how to relate to all of them in a workable way, ACT style, and in a way that helps you be who you want to be.

4. The Richness of Your Precious Values

In Chapter 13, What Are Your Precious Values?, and Chapter 15, Important Questions, Important Answers, we looked at how our values shape our existence and define the direction we take for our lives. We agreed that our values are not our likes or preferences, our goals, our feelings, or our desire to avoid certain feelings.

Moving forward, I strongly encourage you (as my mentor would say when emphasizing something very important) to keep in mind that every single choice you make – how you connect with others, how you talk to people when you're cranky, how you choose your next project or your next trip – is more than just a decision; it's an opportunity to live your values and be who you want to be.

When we fail to keep our values in mind, we move through life as if we're on a freeway without signposts; we end up somewhere but not necessarily where we wanted to go. We may experience many fun, exciting, and pleasurable moments on the way, but our lives are about more than the entertaining, cute, and silly stuff we encounter; our lives are about doing what matters and being who we want to be every step of the way. There is nothing wrong with enjoying yourself, of course – I'm not trying to start the anti-fun movement – but would you like your epitaph to read *Here lies [insert your name]. [Your name] was very busy searching for entertainment and having fun every day*?

I'm not saying that to live a values-based life you need to give up all your pleasurable, enjoyable, and gratifying activities – not at all. But I am saying that life is more than that. Of course, I don't mean to impose anything on you. I can only honestly tell you that the sense of vitality that comes from doing what matters deeply to you, even when dreams don't come true, life gets harsh, and unfair things happen, is refreshing; it keeps you going and gives you an internal sense of peace and comfort.

To recap, the principles of the workability game are: (1) acknowledge the dynamic nature of your mind, (2) accept the true essence of workability, (3) pay attention to the choices you make, and (4) hold on to your values.

I invite you to hold these principles as close as possible; in fact, it might help to get them tattooed somewhere. Just kidding, of course – although it wouldn't hurt to take these principles to heart in any way you want or can. They will help you cultivate a deep sense of inner fulfillment, well-being, and peace without having to depend on things outside yourself, outcomes, or others' validation to feel that you're worthy.

20 Playing It

I don't watch a lot of TV – in fact, I didn't have a TV for seven years – but I absolutely love to watch movies and documentaries. It's one of my favorite things to do: it's soothing, it's a nice break, and it takes my mind in new and interesting directions.

Believe it or not, sometimes I'll watch a movie over three or four days; other times, I'll rewatch a movie a couple of times. And from time to time, I get into watching TV show reruns.

I recently watched a few cooking shows; even though my cooking skills are not the most sophisticated ones, I sometimes find them entertaining, and I still have hopes that, someday, over the rainbow, I'll cook many delicious and sophisticated meals.

While watching these cooking shows, I couldn't stop thinking about how some of the participants had dedicated their careers to creating delicious flavors, mouthwatering dishes, and beautiful presentations of food. And for some of them, you could clearly see that their love of cooking was not just a career or a hobby, but a personal value. They were committed to creating a form of art with their food – from the development of recipes to the selection of ingredients to the food preparation.

You see, playing the workability game is less like preparing a single meal and more like deciding to eat healthy, nutritious, and wholesome food on a regular basis. And like any game, there is no one single thing to do but rather a continuation of things.

Here is how you play the workability game:

(a) You recognize your choice points.

   In Chapter 19, Learning About It, you read that it's super-important to keep an eye out for any form of fear-based reaction to the possibility of things going wrong or mistakes happening; harsh criticisms about not being good enough; ruling-thoughts about how you should always do things the right way or what success looks like; and urges to push yourself as hard as you used to before you learned to check what works for you and what won't work in the long run. These are important choice points because they usually go undetected and unchecked and perpetuate unworkable perfectionistic behaviors.

I needed to make them clear so you can easily recognize them.
To recognize your choice points you can ask yourself questions like:

- Am I acting out of a fear of making mistakes?
- Am I acting to protect myself from not being good enough or from any other story?
- Am I acting based on ruling-thoughts such as *should*, *ought*, *always*, and *either-or*?
- Am I acting based on a push to do things relentlessly without checking what's important in the long run?

(b) You go back to your values.

When encountering a choice point, you ask yourself, *What's truly important to me right now? How do I want to show up in this moment? How do I want to relate to myself?*

Every time you check your personal values, you're taking steps toward living a life with intention and fulfillment.

(c) You radically accept that your dynamic mind is a busy one.

As you know by now, every time you pursue your dreams, goals, and aspirations with the degree of care you give to things that are important to you, your dynamic mind will come armed with a lot of thoughts, options, worries, and "what-ifs." It's not your fault or your mind's fault; it's just the nature of our protective and active minds.

(d) You check what game you're playing.

In Chapter 6, How Come You Care So Much?, we came to terms with the fact that high-achieving actions don't just appear from one day to the next but instead are historically persistent, tenacious behaviors that have been reinforced hundreds of times throughout your life. It's not your fault; the behaviors came about through a combination of personal history, learnings, upbringing, and having a sensitivity to caring deeply about things.

And that's why it is important for you to regularly check which game you are playing. You can ask yourself these questions:

- In this moment, am I playing the workability game, or am I playing that "doing things right and perfectly, no matter what" game?
- In this situation, am I playing the game of doing what works, or am I playing the game of pushing myself all the way without checking in to see what's important in the long term?
- In this conversation, am I playing the workability game, or am I playing the game of being the "perfect" friend that always pleases others?
- In this project, am I playing the workability game, or am I playing the game of always giving my best without checking to see how other areas of my life are being affected?

Playing the workability game is tremendously important because it offers a way to do things your way, be yourself, and live a purposeful life. You will end up feeling inspired every morning, you'll be open to what comes your way each day, and you'll feel fulfilled when the day ends.

When you look back on your life, you'll be able to say, "I lived a life worth living," and, more importantly, you'll see the people you love next to you.

21 Committing to It

You just finished reading about the principles of the workability game – how to play it and what it's about – and since it's a game, and games have winners and losers, you may be curious about a few things, like how to win, who wins and who loses, what's the prize for winning, or what happens when you lose.

Here is my response: when playing the workability game, there are no winners or losers because no one wins parenting, friendship, health, relationships, or spirituality. The workability game is a way of living a values-based life – a life in which you're striving to be the person you want to be in all areas, all the time, and no matter who you're with, the time of the day, or where you live. It's not a one-and-done move, but a constant effort and a series of regular choices you make. For instance, if I want to be a caring daughter, then checking on my mom, visiting with her, being present when we're together, making a meal for her, or going out together are all ways to show her that I care. But I'm never done. I'm always making moves toward my value of being a caring daughter. We're always working toward our values.

Your prize is the fulfillment, contentedness, satisfaction, and incredible sense of vitality that comes from doing all the things you do in service of your values. Things may go wrong, things will be out of your control, and you may experience setbacks, disappointments, and frustrations, but when you're clear that you did what you could to get closer to the life you wanted to live, then you can never lose.

A values-based life is not defined by how things unfold (because we just don't know how things will go) or by chasing feelings (the perfect and right feeling) or by seeking external validation (that's not possible all the time), but by choosing how you want to live your life and making the most of it every moment you're alive.

You see, what's very humbling about playing the workability game as a way of living life is that one way or another you need to acknowledge that there are many things you don't have control over. No matter how hard you push yourself, how many nights you don't sleep while pursuing a project, or how much you pay attention to what you're saying, how you look, or what you're thinking, none of these efforts can guarantee you the outcome you want – it sucks, it's true, and it can be humbling to accept that reality.

DOI: 10.4324/9781003083153-26

In fact, it's that strong attachment to outcomes, to rules about how things should be, how you should behave, and how to avoid failure, that keeps you stuck in a loop of ineffective perfectionistic actions.

To play the workability game, you need to focus on what deeply matters to you, and you need to gauge the workability of every action you take based on whether it takes you closer to or further from your values; that's true workability, and that's your true meter in life.

And, as with any game – and a life worth living – there are complicated moments. How do I live my value of being a caring daughter with my mom if I cannot take time off from work? How do I show up for her when she's preaching for hours about something I should have done? What happens when I'm stressed about a work situation and my mom is sharing all her health struggles with me? How do I show up for my mom when I'm feeling a bit trapped in the conversation?

In complicated moments like these, you can predict that your mind will bring up old behaviors, old actions, and old ways of thinking. That's what your dynamic mind is supposed to do: recall old strategies to minimize the stress of the here and now. It will push you to do the same old, same old behaviors without checking what works for you in the present moment.

In each one of those problematic moments, you're at a crossroads between new workable behaviors and old ones – between new behaviors that encourage you to do things your way without pushing yourself toward burnout, and old behaviors that push you to show up perfectly in all that you do regardless of how it's working in your life. For example, if you want to show up for your kids and have regular family dinners, but also feel the pull to stay at work for a couple extra hours so you can manage your fear of failing. Or if you're preparing your outfit for the day, but have an urge to spend hours and hours changing the outfit to manage the distress that comes when looking at your body. Or if you're sharing with friends how much you dislike a political candidate, but notice an itch to go along with their opinions so you don't feel embarrassed. Or if you need to a buy a new coffee machine, but feel the pull to research relentlessly in order to make the best decision and avoid regretting it later.

It's when facing those crossroads that you need to check what works for you in that particular situation, ACT style, and which action will take you closer to your values. That's the most important question to ask yourself. And, trust me, you will face many crossroads, through no fault of your own; it's just life.

Playing the workability game is never going to be a flawless path, free of crossroads, messiness, or challenges. But if you choose to play it, then you are also invited to make a choice to come back to your values, time and again, over and over. No one can make the decision for you; it's a personal choice.

Within ACT, when we talk about commitment, we're not referring to automatically doing what your mind asks you to do or what your fears of making mistakes, not being good enough, or things going wrong demand that you do. We're referring to making a personal commitment to be who you want to be every moment you're alive on this planet.

Committing to do this – to be who you want to be – means committing to playing the workability game, all the way, and checking in with what matters in each moment and with full intention. It's about recommitting hundreds of times to the stuff that matters to you. It's about acknowledging when you're stuck, appreciating the difficulty of a given situation, and checking again to see what's deeply important to you. It's about mining the power of your perfectionistic and high-achieving behaviors without losing yourself.

And from the bottom of my heart, and in full honesty, I can tell you that life is much, much, much better, richer, and more gratifying when you're playing the workability game with full commitment. For real.

(Psst, you can get a single-sheet summary of the workability game from the page "ACT for perfectionism and high-achieving actions" on my personal website https://www.thisisdoctorz.com/act-for-perfectionism-and-high-achieving-behaviors/.)

Section V

Pause and Play

Yay, you just made it to a very special section of this book!

Let's do a mini recap before jumping into it. In Section IV, The Workability Game, you learned that, to play the workability game and live a fulfilling life, you need to keep in mind four key principles: (1) the dynamic nature of your mind, (2) the true essence of workability, (3) the choices you make, and (4) the richness of your precious values. In other words, you need to keep in mind that your mind will always do its own minding, what works is what takes you closer to your values, you can make choices to handle every situation you encounter and all the thoughts, feelings, and sensations that come with them, and your values can always guide every action you take. It's like these four principles are the basis of your new mindset to keep nurturing those perfectionistic actions!

But having a new mindset is not enough. You need to know what to do in your day-to-day life. So, in Chapter 20, Playing It, you learned that to play the workability game you need to catch your choice points, go back to your values, radically accept that your dynamic mind is a busy one, and check often what game you're playing. So basically, when moving through your day and encountering tricky, anxious, and frustrating moments, you can ask yourself what's the driver of your actions: is it the fear of making mistakes, is it to protect yourself from not being good enough in any form, is it because of some ruling-thoughts?

And in Chapter 21, Committing to It, we established that playing the workability game is like making a personal decision of going back to your values, over an over, no matter what, and committing and recommitting to be the person you want to be every single moment you're on this earth without hurting yourself or your relationships.

Now you're 50 percent ready to maximize, amplify, and enjoy all the benefits of high-achieving actions and live a life worth living; in this section, you will learn the other 50 percent you need: micro-skills to make solid moves every day.

You can open up any chapter, anytime, and you'll find something helpful right away. Each chapter is somewhat independent of the others, but they're all related. Of course, I encourage you to read all of them, one after the other, and try on all these new micro-skills. Some of the chapters are playful and lighthearted, others are more on the reflective side

DOI: 10.4324/9781003083153-27

of things, but I like to think that all of them are like doors opening into a spectacular view that enables you to be who you are and appreciate who you are, allows you to see further and further, and opens up the possibility for new ways of living life. At the end of each chapter, you will find a mini-section called "Pause and Play" with reflective questions, how-tos, and, micro-skills that you can put into action right away.

My hope is that you will make each one of these micro-skills yours by trying them, seeing how they work, and checking how they relate to doing things that matter to you to the best of your abilities.

One last thing: don't rush through these chapters. Give yourself some time to really make these skills yours!

22 The Great Escape

On a sunny day, I was riding my bike on a narrow street when the bright T-shirt of a pedestrian caught my attention. In a hot-pink color, the word "ESCAPE" was printed in a modern font on a navy blue background. You couldn't miss it. My eyes didn't, and my mind didn't either.

Hundreds of books, movies, stories, and tales have explored the topic of what we are naturally drawn to and what we avoid, what we face and what we hide from, what we lean toward and what we run away from. You see, we humans, we're not designed to hurt, suffer, or be in pain; our evolutionary makeup has shown us over and over that when experiencing any form of discomfort, we run away from it at the speed of light. No human being will spontaneously say, "I like this painful experience." That's just not in our disposition.

Our disposition is to perform a great escape every time we're hurt.

In Section II, Unpacking Your Personal History, we tapped into the complexity of caring so deeply for something. In Chapter 4, Flipping the Coin, we explored the fact that it's human to hold onto rules about how things need to be when something is important to us; we get scared about things going wrong, we're anxious about things being forgotten, we're worried about looking like failures, and we relate to ourselves in very harsh ways when things don't go as planned.

None of these experiences sounds fun, exciting, or appealing; in fact, they all sound embarrassing, and like the perfect excuses to run away as soon as possible. But when I say "run away," I'm referring not only to the behaviors related to getting out of a situation or physically removing yourself from one, but also to the tricky versions of "running away" from the yucky feelings that come along in those moments. When you go into runaway mode from those unpleasant feelings, you do a bunch of things that you're familiar with: overpreparing, overworking, overthinking, overplanning, or overdoing things and many, many more.

Playing a long workability game, then, means keeping an eye on those choice points that will come your way one after another.

> Richard very much appreciated aesthetics since he was a little boy. When he and his girlfriend, Jessica, decided to move in together, he was thrilled and was very much looking forward to sharing his life

DOI: 10.4324/9781003083153-28

with her. They both agreed that they were ready to take their relationship to the next level after dating for two years. They liked the same TV shows, both loved dogs, had similar taste in movies, were kind to others, and had a true friendship as the basis for their romantic relationship.

After ten days of packing and unpacking, cleaning, rearranging furniture, and eating delivery food almost every night, Jessica was fully moved into Richard's apartment. Richard was excited and committed to be a caring, loving, and supportive boyfriend for Jessica; he deeply wanted to be a "good boyfriend" for Jessica. A couple of weeks after their move, Richard started noticing how annoying it was to see dirty dishes in the sink almost every night, used coffee mugs all over the apartment, shoes spread around the living room, and the occasional sock he found in the couch.

Richard didn't say anything to Jessica because he didn't want to come across as a nagging or annoying boyfriend. He thought that saying something to Jessica about it wouldn't be consistent with "being a good boyfriend" because good boyfriends are supposed to be tolerant, understanding, and accepting of their partners. After a month of hoping that things would change on their own, Richard found himself doing the dishes almost every night, picking up clothes, and cleaning the apartment before going to work. He realized that keeping the apartment as he liked it resulted in him having less time to go to the office early, go for runs on weekdays, or just catch up on the phone with friends.

Richard knew that keeping a clean, organized, and well-arranged home was very important to him, and he also knew that relationships require sacrifices, adjustments, and accommodations. Sometimes, when doing his regular cleaning before going to work, he felt reassured that he was being a good and understanding boyfriend and felt better about himself. Other times, when he felt annoyed, unhappy, or resentful about taking on these tasks, he reminded himself that he wanted to be a good boyfriend to Jessica at all times, including when dealing with the messiness of the apartment.

To the eyes of outsiders, Richard's responses might seem appropriate. But what would have happened if he hadn't cleaned up Jessica's coffee mugs, dishes, and clothes? Quite likely, he would have felt frustrated, angry, and irritated – and also concerned, nervous, and anxious about offending Jessica, disappointing her, or acting as a nagging boyfriend. Richard didn't want to feel any of those uncomfortable feelings and preferred the good ones that came with taking care of the tasks himself. Richard was performing an escape with his actions, one after another. All of Richard's responses worked right away – as it happens when you avoid triggering situations – so he didn't feel any of the yucky stuff he was worried about – but, in the long run, other feelings emerged.

It feels good to get things done. It feels good to do what you need to do to manage yucky feelings, as Richard was doing. It feels good to do what seems to be the perfect response. But – and this is another big "but" – all those good feelings that come when you escape from, shun, avoid are fleeting ones, not permanent ones. It's a matter of time until you will feel all those feelings you're running away from.

> **Pause and Play**
>
> Playing the workability game requires that you handle all types of feelings – that you sit with them and learn from them without running away or wrestling with them and without checking how they really work for you.
> Here is what you can do:
>
> - Do an inventory of all strategies you use (*) to manage the emotional discomfort that comes your way when there's the possibility of making errors, exposing flaws, being seen as a failure, or being perceived in a way that doesn't feel true.
>
> (*) You can get a checklist of the most common strategies that people with high-achieving and perfectionistic actions rely on to handle emotional distress from the page "ACT for perfectionism and high-achieving actions" on my personal website https://www.thisisdoctorz.com/act-for-perfectionism-and-high-achieving-behaviors/

23 Fleeting Feelings

It's quite likely that, every time you were doing something that mattered to you and doing it as it mattered to you, you took great care to protect yourself from feeling those yucky emotions, just as Richard did in the previous chapter. If you did an inventory of all these subtle, private, or public actions you used to manage all those fears of messing things up, not being good enough, failing, or things going wrong, you might notice that they all have worked right away, like in the blink of an eye, and that they all feel good, relieving, and soothing almost immediately. But all those good feelings that come afterward – after relying on those strategies – they all create the artificial experience that you have control of those yucky emotions and that the only way to handle them is by using those strategies over and over. Oh boy!

Sorry for repeating myself here but, all these good feelings are short-lived, momentary, and passing ones. Like shoes wear out, like waves in the ocean dissolve, like the flavors of our food disappear, our uncomfortable feelings, and all feelings, come and go.

All of our emotions are temporary states. Researchers tell us that our feelings last an average of seven minutes, including the so-called positive feelings and the uncomfortable ones too; they arise and disappear, only to arise and disappear again and again.

Check for yourself: have you ever felt happy for 24 hours straight? Did you ever have a full day when you felt excitement non-stop? After you've been with a person romantically for a while, do you still feel butterflies in your stomach every single time you see them? Of course, there are moments when you feel really good about a particular project, task, relationship, or conversation, but do all those feelings remain the same in intensity and duration as time unfolds?

Let's consider uncomfortable feelings. If you've ever had a panic attack, you know how scary it can be. You have difficulty breathing, your heart beats fast, your body feels hot, and it feels like these sensations will go on forever. You may even think you're dying, going crazy, or having a heart attack. But all panic sensations have a beginning and an end. In fact, I cannot tell you how many times my clients end up in the emergency room only to be told that it's a panic attack, that they need to see a psychologist, and that there is nothing the doctors can do in that moment.

Eventually, all our feelings cease. But what happens when you are busy...

Chasing Good and Perfect Feelings

Let's think about a couple of scenarios: let's say that you're preparing an essay to apply for a graduate program; so with your best intentions, you make sure to use the right words, check and recheck the essay structure almost every night, ask others to read it multiple times, reread it yourself before going to sleep, and even when going to the gym, you think on a nonstop reel about the best way to show in that application who you are and why you should be accepted. All these actions make total sense because you're pursuing something important and it feels good to work hard to accomplish your goals. In this scenario, you're also managing the distress that comes with applying to grad school but doing what you need to be doing to increase the likelihood of your application being accepted.

Now, let's imagine that you're feeling worried about the car you need to buy. You go over in your mind all the possibilities you may encounter in the future and how you will handle them: what if I move to another city? Would this car be safe for driving long distances? Could I sell this car later on? What if I have a family down the road – would this car fit me and my family? Would my parents feel safe in this car? If I go camping, would I be able to hook a van to it? Would I feel safe with children in this car? Can I go skiing and snowboarding with this car? You might try to answer each one of these questions in order to ensure that you make the best decision. Otherwise, you might regret it later and feel bad about it. And when solving, researching, and addressing each one of those possibilities impeccably, you feel good about it. In this situation, you managed that uneasiness that came with buying a car by answering each one those worries.

If you look back at those scenarios, in both of them, you handled your internal distress by doing a bunch of things: re-checking, searching for information, consulting with others, thinking about it, and many more. All these actions reinforce, maintain, and support the evidence that the only way to handle the inner discomfort you feel when doing things you care about is by doing them perfectly; and if you repeat that cycle hundreds of times, then your mind is learning that the only way to manage emotional discomfort is by chasing those good feelings.

Building a fulfilling life and playing the workability game is more than chasing a fleeting good feeling or a comfy emotion; it's more than managing internal distress with the perfect behaviors.

Pause and Play

You need to step back and learn to have all of your emotions – the fleeting ones, the easy ones, the enjoyable ones, the overwhelming ones, and the chronically annoying ones. All of them. And learning to have them means that you intentionally choose to be aware of and awake to all your feelings. It means saying yes to whatever feeling comes your way. Here is what you can start doing:

- Notice your feelings as they are and describe them to yourself. You can say, "here is my fear of being an impostor. Here is my fear about being seen as a failure. Here is my discomfort about things potentially going bad. Here is my stress about people rejecting me. Here is the fear of looking overweight."

- Telling yourself, "here is this awful feeling. I hate feeling angry" is not making room for those feelings. Judging and criticizing your feelings is not saying yes to them. Intellectualizing about your emotions is not learning to have them.

24 Seizing and Freezing

I'm going to say three words: check, coffee, and mouse. Now I ask you to come up with a story that includes these three words; it doesn't have to be a sophisticated story but just a story that connects those three words. I promise you that I have no intention of wasting your time; as silly as this exercise sounds, it's related to this chapter. Trust me!

What story did you come up with?

Here is what my mind invented:

I was making my morning coffee, enjoying the smell, imagining the taste of it, and listening to the sound of the coffee machine, when Sally, the mouse of the house, ran quickly toward me. As she got closer and closer, I could see she was asking for something. What does she want? I wondered. Carefully, I held Sally with both of my hands and brought her to my shoulder, while still waiting for the coffee to be ready. Sally is quite playful, so she moved around on my shoulder but balanced her body so she wouldn't fall. I poured my coffee and started sipping while moving around the kitchen. But while I was moving, Sally kept moving too, as if she were trying to guide me toward something. I kept moving, and Sally kept moving with me. I sat down to read the news, and little Sally moved toward my lap, as she always does. I sat, relaxed, and grabbed the newspaper. But while I was stretching to reach the newspaper, a check that was sitting on the table fell down to the floor in slow motion. As the check fell down, little Sally jumped from my lap toward it. As if it were a magic carpet, she rode the check until they both landed on the kitchen floor.

Is this ability to connect, associate, organize, classify, and cluster information a new one? The answer is no. As you'll recall from Chapter 11, Personal Narratives, and Chapter 19, Learning About It, our minds are constantly creating narratives, linking one thing with another, and making connections, whether we notice these activities or not. This is the same whether we're experiencing challenges, hardship, and uncomfortable situations or amazing, joyful, and fulfilling experiences.

You may wonder: why is she saying the same thing again? Here is my response: in the hundreds of hours I've worked with clients prone to

DOI: 10.4324/9781003083153-30

high-achieving behaviors, from the 7-year-old to the 50-year-old and everyone in between, I have heard over and over how their dynamic minds have lives of their own, to a maximum level. Sometimes, I think of perfectionism as an overthinking problem. Not surprising, right?

You can try another exercise if you want. Grab your cell phone, scroll through your pictures, and choose one of your favorites. Don't get too distracted trying to find the perfect image; just find one that you love to look at from time to time. Take a couple of moments to describe three characteristics of that image – the color of an object, the type of clothing a person is wearing, and so on. Next, just let your attention follow what your mind comes up with.

What did you notice.

That's just another snippet of what our minds do in one brief moment. Imagine what they do in a whole day.

Wherever we go, we take with us our incessant, unstoppable, and unrelenting minds, which come up with all manner of thoughts, hypotheses, wishes, dreams, obsessions, worries, fantasies, solutions, biases, and so on. I'm afraid I could write a whole book on the content of our dynamic minds. I'm not sure my publisher would be up for it.

Is it possible that we take our dynamic minds too seriously and overestimate their ability to judge what's true?

But, how often do we stick to our guns, to our beliefs, opinions, and knowledge, and live by them without doubting, questioning, or challenging them?

How often do we prefer the ease of hanging onto old views over the difficulty of grappling with new ways of understanding reality, ourselves, and others? Why do we occasionally prefer the comfort of what we know over the discomfort of doubting what we know? Why do we do that?

Psychologists have called this process seizing and freezing (Kruglanski & Webster, 1996), which basically means that, sometimes, we may seize on information that appears early and freeze on it, despite future data showing us something different. When we quickly accept something as the truth, we reduce, minimize, or get rid of the discomfort that comes from not knowing. It feels good to know (you can listen to episode 25 on uncertainty in the website www.playingitsafe.zone).

This chapter is an invitation for you to acknowledge – once again – the busy nature of your mind and an opportunity for you to reflect on whether the content it comes up with – e.g. rules about high–achieving actions, the meaning of mistakes, stories about errors, what failure represents – is the absolute truth and whether you're seizing and freezing as your mind gets busy generating new content.

Pause and Play

Moving forward, imagine that your dynamic mind is broadcasting all types of content nonstop, then check for these things:

- If your dynamic mind is broadcasting something useful, tune in to it!
- If your dynamic mind is broadcasting something unhelpful that takes you apart from what's deeply important to you – your values – tune in to what you're doing at that moment.
- If your dynamic mind is pushing you to do something as you always do – check if you're seizing and freezing.

25   Overly Protective Friends

Let me share a brief story with you.

> On a Tuesday morning, the doorbell to my apartment rang. I walked down the stairs and heard someone's footsteps walking away. I opened the door, and there was a package on the doormat. I picked it up and noticed the slight heft of it. As I opened the box, I heard the crinkly sounds of the purple paper that was covering a large green book. I was now holding *Veganomicon*, a beautiful cookbook full of pictures, basic cooking information, and personal stories. As my fingers flipped through the pages of recipes, Black-Bean Soup, Broccoli-Millet Croquettes, Panko-Stuffed Mushrooms, and Creamed Corn, my mind was saying, "Oh boy. It's such a beautiful gift. Wow, it's gorgeous, this recipe looks amazing . . . and it's so intimidating too. I wish I had the skills. They make it look so easy to cook these recipes, but it's so challenging. They always say the recipes are for 'everyday meals,' but that's not true for me. What if even when using this beautiful cookbook, I still make tasteless dishes? Will I ever be able to cook more than my plain go-to meals? What if I put hours of work in the kitchen and then no one likes the meals? Oh boy, it will be – once again – a proof of my incompetence in the kitchen."

How many moments like this have you experienced? Not necessarily related to cooking, but moments in which your mind shouted all kinds of doubts, worries, and concerns about stuff you wanted to do, random things, and even unimportant decisions you needed to make?

Our dynamic minds have many functions. I'm not going to bore you with all of them right now, but for the purposes of this book, I want to revisit their protective function.

When I was turning the pages of *Veganomicon*, my mind was going on and on about my cooking struggles. But it was also trying to prevent me from having a disaster in the kitchen, feeling disappointed by my culinary skills, feeling ashamed of having a Latin background and not being talented in the kitchen.

This may sound strange or like a bunch of rubbish to you, but the reality is that my mind was acting – once again – like an overly protective, overly caring, and overly compassionate friend. Stay with me for a moment. Think about all those times when your mind came up with messages about things going wrong, a situation having a bad outcome, people rejecting you, or your integrity being questioned. It may feel as if your mind is your enemy, as if you're carrying an adversary within you, but is that really the case? Is it really that your mind works super-hard to harm, hurt, and shame you?

If you recall, in Chapter 6, How Come You Care So Much?, we established that if our dynamic minds intentionally wanted to harm us, our ancestors wouldn't have survived. We wouldn't have developed as a species or evolved to where we are today. The cavewomen and cavemen couldn't have handled all the complex situations they were exposed to without having dynamic minds working to protect them in every step they took and anticipating every possible thing that could go wrong. Without our brains foreseeing these potential threats, we wouldn't be here.

It just so happens that, over the course of time, our dynamic minds have grown a collection of messages to guard us from bad things happening and to keep us from making mistakes or embarrassing ourselves; these messages vary from soft in tone (e.g., you need bring the umbrella in case it rains) to mild (e.g., if you don't study hard enough, you will fail your law exam) to tough (e.g., are you an idiot?). But our dynamic minds haven't adjusted to the time we're living in, and they make prediction errors.

For instance, your mind may always perceive the sound of a helicopter as a threat (even if the helicopter is carrying someone to the hospital), may anticipate that people will laugh at you if you make a mistake (even though much of the time other people are not paying attention to us), or may assume that a recipe you cook from *Veganomicon* will be tasteless (even though you have had some success with making it).

The list of examples of how our dynamic minds try to protect us is limitless and unique to each one of us, But at the end of the day, our minds are less like adversaries and more like one of those friends who try to be super-helpful but end up making things harder for us.

> **Pause and Play**
>
> To play the workability game you have to keep present that your dynamic mind is genuinely trying to be helpful, but it's not always successful.
>
> This week, when your mind comes at you with criticism, judgment, or unfair verdicts about who you are and what you're doing, saying, or feeling, ask yourself:
>
> - What is my dynamic mind trying to protect me from right now?
> - What's the potential disaster my dynamic mind is warning me about?
> - What's the feeling my dynamic mind is loudly shielding me from?

26   To Buy or Not to Buy?

Chapter by chapter, you have read about, and experienced through brief exercises, how our minds have lives of their own.

Sometimes our dynamic minds are useful: they show us what direction to go to find our favorite restaurant, come up with ideas for our next trip, guide us in our next career move, or alert us to danger. And thousands of times, our dynamic minds go to places we wish we didn't have to go. Oh boy, what are we going to do with our dynamic minds?!

Our thoughts, all of them – including memories, images, and all the other forms of mental representation our minds come up with – have a feeling that comes with them and an action associated with them. They want us to do something, to take action, and that action is usually either internal or external; either we respond to our thinking with more thinking or we respond to it with an observable action.

Interestingly, even though we have little control over our thoughts – e.g. don't think of your toe – we invest tons of time, energy, and effort in them, as if they had authority over us and as if we're defined by them. Of course, that makes sense given that for hundreds of years, especially in the Western world, we have been influenced by rationalism, but are we really defined by the countless images, memories, hypotheses, worries, theories, and stories generated in our dynamic minds?

Is it 100 percent accurate that what you believe becomes your reality?

Is it correct that what you visualize with your mind becomes your life?

How can you live peacefully with the confounding and marvelous thought-making and storytelling machines of your dynamic mind?

How can you find stillness in your life amid the rushing thoughts?

How can you do what you care deeply about when your mind starts its relentless activities as soon as you open your eyes?

The key is to choose what thoughts you want to respond to and what thoughts you need to let go without getting caught on them.

Pause and Play

When your dynamic mind gets loud and bossy, starts acting like a dictator, and demands you do all types of private and public behaviors to manage the fear of making mistakes or being a failure, instead of arguing with it, judging yourself, or judging your mind for behaving that way:

- Let your mind do its own thinking: watch it, observe it, and notice it.
- Accept that your mind is broadcasting.
- Hold all that broadcasting noise lightly, as stuff that shows up in your mind, but not as full reality.
- Take a deep breath to the count of three and shift your attention to what's in front of you.

27 Hold Them Lightly, Really!

On Saturday evening, as George was preparing his traditional birthday dinner, he grabbed the phone to invite his best friends over the next day. Phil, his partner, kept asking him to hang up the phone so they could chat, but George wanted to talk with his friends first and then chat with Phil. Phil insisted, so George quickly sent a group text to his friends about the birthday gathering, but got frustrated over Phil's insistence on chatting. Phil waited until he was done and then said: "As a birthday surprise, I had booked us a trip to Hawaii for tomorrow so you could relax, swim in the ocean, and eat seafood. I thought it would be a great place to celebrate your birthday; I wanted it to be special since it's the first year we're celebrating it together."

George gave Phil a hug, smiled softly, and despite his efforts, his forehead showed some notorious wrinkles. Phil asked what was wrong. George took a breath, and then said, "I have always done my birthday dinners with my friends. You shouldn't have booked something and paid for it without consulting me first. This is my tradition. It's important for me to do something with my friends for special occasions, like my birthday; they're my lifelong friends."

Our wonderful mental rubrics, oh boy! You see, there is nothing sinful with our mind generating many ruling-thoughts – see Chapter 10, Mental Rubrics, and Chapter 19, Learning About It – but what gets us in trouble and takes us far away from what's important to us is quickly going along with each one of them. And, of course, when you genuinely care about something, feel invested, or are indisputably pursuing something, like George, your dynamic mind will keep your ruling-thoughts at the top of mind for you. No matter the occasion, where you are, or who you're with, your mind will make sure you pay attention to those deep-rooted ruling-thoughts.

Since you are more attuned to high-achieving actions, you may be more or less familiar with some of these ruling-thoughts:

- I should always know what I'm talking about.
- I need to make sure I don't hurt people's feelings.
- It's important for me to be fair at all times.
- It's up to me to always have the right responses.
- If it's not done right, it's not worth doing.

DOI: 10.4324/9781003083153-33

- Mistakes are a no-no; I'm the only one who can do this correctly.
- If I don't work hard, that means I'm being lazy and not giving my best.
- Bad outcomes are not an option.
- The more information I gather, the better it is.
- Not maintaining my goals or standards reflects on my character, personality, and values.

. . . and probably countless other variations on these ruling-thought themes.

Our minds are extremely talented at holding onto thoughts with white knuckles – rules, in particular – because sometimes those ruling-thoughts help us accomplish what we need, want, and hope for. You may feel accomplished, appreciated, and even excited when going along with those rules, which is totally fine; the question is, what's the payoff for pursuing those feelings in the long run?

Going back to George, he didn't mean to be ungrateful to Phil or to disregard his efforts. It just so happened that George was very, very, very attached to the thought of "creating annual birthday memories with his friends" as part of his value of "having real connections with others." Because this value was important to him, he started a tradition with his close friends, created memories with his friends as much as he could, and showed up for his friendships as much as he could. If you were to ask George's friends about what type of friend George is, they may say, "a loyal one."

It's not your fault that your brain is a creature of habit and that it resists change, especially after you have benefited from some of the actions that result from ruling-thoughts, as was the case with George. But it's important to remember that our lives move, change, and shift – look at your life and all the changes you have gone through! In order to live a better life, a life that you're proud of, you need another micro-skill: holding those ruling-thoughts lightly.

Pause and Play

You can feel very hooked on all those ruling-thoughts: ought, should, must, always, either-or, strong preferences. But, to turn the difficulties that come with high achievements into opportunities to build a life that matters to you, you need to:

- Take stock of all your ruling-thoughts that you can think of.
- Write them down.
- Give them names.

    (e.g., the master musts; the impossible rules; the extreme thoughts).

- Catch them as they occur throughout the day.
- Check what's truly important to you when any of those ruling-thoughts show up.

28 99 Percent

On a Sunday afternoon, after having a nice day hiking under a warm and bright sun, eating grilled veggies and sautéed mushrooms, and chatting with my neighbor, I changed my clothes to head to my regular gathering with my mentor.

I rode my bike to the restaurant in the noisy streets of a university town. While securing my bike to a pole, I saw there were two little kids staring at me, then we all exchanged a goofy smile. I walked into a restaurant full of high ceilings, rustic old wood beams, large hanging plants, and the smell of a home-cooked meal.

A smiling waitress walked me to our table. As I waited for my mentor to arrive, I ordered a beer. A bright, golden beer arrived and, with it, the smell of a rich, earthy drink.

I held the glass, lifted it to my mouth, took a sip, and enjoyed the sharp flavor of a light, creamy, and smooth beer.

What happened when you read the description of this memory of mine? What did you notice? Perhaps your dynamic mind imagined the scene and visualized the restaurant, the glass of beer, the high ceilings, and the smiling waitress. Perhaps you smelled, saw, and even felt the flavor of the beer.

Now, imagine that, instead, I shared a memory about the time I walked into a park and bird poop landed on my forehead; or about the scary movie I couldn't watch because it was so violent; or about the time I accidentally cooked a gazpacho; or about the nights when my sleep is interrupted three or four times because of insomnia. Quite likely your mind would have imagined elements of each one of those scenes as if you were living them, as if they were your memories. And that's the extraordinary power of symbols.

After we're born, and for a very short period of time, we learn about the world through what we see, touch, smell, taste, and hear. But when we enter the world of symbols – anything that refers to something else – like letters, words, sentences, images, associations, and all the connections that can be made about anything and everything, we also enter a world in which every symbol our mind comes up with has the power to create an experience.

DOI: 10.4324/9781003083153-34

Our minds are constantly constructing, adding, connecting, changing, and modifying our symbolic world. Can you imagine in this moment all the information and symbols you have in your dynamic mind?

This idea that *symbols have the power to create experiences* can sound a bit confusing, so hear me out a little bit. When you were reading my description of sipping a beer, you may have had an experience of it, even though you weren't there – because words have power. Here is another example: you can read about, talk about, and share your opinions about a movie, about the Sahara desert, or about your favorite dish, and each experience will be totally different from watching the movie, being in the Sahara desert, or eating your favorite dish. So, in a nutshell, symbols – words, letters, imaginings, and associations – are very different from experiences and yet, when we have them, we confuse them with direct experiences.

One more example: when you have thoughts like, "If I don't do things perfectly, that means I'm giving myself a pass to be lazy; if I don't pay attention to important details – nitty-gritty types of things – I'll radically fail; my successes, achievements, and accomplishments speak to how worthy I am," it's not the same as giving yourself a break, failing, or being worthy as a human being.

Sometimes you may have physical sensations connected to the words or images in your head – as when reading about my memory – but physical sensations stemming from mental representations – symbols – are not the same as having direct experiences. Now, can you imagine all the times we may have confused symbols with experiences?

Ninety-nine percent of the time, we take our minds very seriously. We confuse symbols with experiences. We take all types of pictures, words, letters or sentences, and related sensations as equal as direct experiences. And while that's natural and to be expected, it's not necessarily helpful when playing a lifelong game.

In ACT, we urge you to keep in mind this ultra-, super-, very important distinction between symbols and direct experiences: when you confuse symbols with experiences, we refer to that process as fusion. When this happens, we say that you're "fused" with those symbols and when distancing yourself from them, we called that process "defusion." In this book, I also refer to fusion as being hooked on thoughts, buying into thoughts, or getting caught on thoughts; and the skills to separate yourself from those thoughts as defusion or unhooking skills.

When you're fused with words or images, you:

- Take all your thoughts as absolute realities
- Take all your thoughts as truth
- Take all your thoughts as important
- Take all your thoughts as commands to behave in a certain way

If I were to take my thoughts of "I'm not-a-writer" as the truth, trust me, you wouldn't be reading this book. You have been learning in different chapters – and will be learning more – different defusion skills to get unhooked, disentangled, and disengaged from all that mind noise that pushes you to make unworkable moves.

> **Pause and Play**
>
> As your dynamic mind continues to create incalculable quantities of words and pictures in your head, and as you have physical sensations of them, keep in mind that not all the content that shows up is true, important, instructive, or real.
>
> When a loud thought pops up in your mind – e.g., I need to check one more time; it's not ready; I need to work harder – ask yourself these questions:
>
> - Have I heard this thought before?
> - Is this an old thought?
> - If I take this thought as fact, does it help me do something that matters deeply to me?
>
> Maybe you can start taking your mind seriously 1 percent of the time.

29 This-Or-That Thoughts

If I don't meet my deadline, then I'll be just as irresponsible as everybody else.
If I don't run today, I'll get fat.
If I tell people that I disagree with their political views, I'll seem rude and ungrateful because they always spend time with me.
Not organizing my books means that I'm lazy.
If I don't work hard on my paper, I won't get the results I want, and that will make me a failure.
If I don't give my best on this project, I'm a loser.
If I don't perform well in this show, my career will be over, and I'll just be a bump on a log.

On a Monday evening, after a full day of sessions, I was sipping a cup of chamomile tea, recalling the hundreds of conversations I had with my clients over the years and remembering all those moments in which I paused, shifted my body a bit, and asked: "Did you notice what your mind just did? Did you pay attention to how your mind, at the speed of light, quickly jumped to a conclusion about how one thing means something else about your character?"

I sometimes call these this-or-that thoughts; other psychologists call them black-and-white thoughts, all-or-nothing thoughts, or polarized thinking. This-or-that thoughts are another type of content that your protective mind thinks of in its attempt to motivate you, to guard you from making a fool of yourself, and to shield you from performing poorly or below your standards. Tough love!

When we're having this-or-that thoughts, our minds insist that there are no shades of gray and jump into extremes. It's like we're either wonderful or horrible, kind or ungrateful, fun to be around or boring. The greatest danger of these thoughts is that they can affect how you think of yourself, how you feel about yourself, and how you treat yourself.

And when we're dealing with high-achieving or perfectionistic actions, it is muuuuuuuuuuuch harder because one mistake, one action that is less than ideal, or one variation from how things are supposed to be somehow means that you're incompetent, unworthy, mediocre, an imbecile, a failure, or any other version of not-good-enough.

DOI: 10.4324/9781003083153-35

Allison, a single mother with two kids, was committed to being strong and available for her kids at all times, given that they had only her as a protective, loving, and caring figure. Between working full-time, preparing meals, driving the kids to school, scheduling doctor's appointments, doing the laundry, returning calls in the middle of the night, and making sure they attended after-school activities, Allison often felt very tired and nervous about dropping the ball. If she found herself saying, "I'm so tired, I don't know if I can do this any longer," she would quickly start thinking of herself as weak.

When the mind grabs onto this-or-that thoughts, it often won't let them go. You may try to argue with the thoughts, but as you know by now, arguing with your mind, while effective at times, is at best a temporary fix. It's only a matter of time until your thoughts come back again, in their ultimate, utmost, and extreme forms.

Catching this-and-that thoughts requires you to be fully present so you don't get lost in them as they quickly arise.

Pause and Play

Try this:

- Take a moment to sit down, grab a piece of paper, and do an inventory of the this-or-that thoughts that your mind usually comes up with.
- How do you see yourself when having those this-or-that thoughts?
- To disentangle yourself from these thoughts when they pop up, make a song out of them. You can come up with your own melody or sing them to the tune of your favorite song.

30 Minding and Unwinding

Our minds do their minding, and we do the unwinding.

Our minds will relentlessly do their minding: thinking and thinking, thinking and thinking again. They come at us unstoppably with content: dreams, jokes to share, memories of past trips, to-do lists, speculations, and so much more. Every person's mind is unique, and yet, all of our minds are busy minds. But as you keep reading and practicing the skills from this book, you'll be better off holding your dynamic mind lightly and unwinding.

So far, you have learned about different micro-skills to handle different types of thoughts. All the skills you have been learning and the ones ahead are all about taking your mind lightly and shifting from being hooked on thoughts to getting yourself unhooked. In this chapter, we'll dive into other defusion micro-skills in great detail so you have more options to handle those tricky thoughts.

But before we move on, here are some important clarifications to make the best of these unhooking skills:

- None of these defusion skills are intended to reduce, minimize, or eliminate the troublesome thoughts, stories, or pictures that show up in your mind.
- You don't need to practice defusion skills with all of your troublesome, uncomfortable, and annoying thoughts – just with the ones that push you to act in ways that are inconsistent with your values and take you far away from who you want to be.
- No defusion skill is infallible, so rather than waiting to experience a decrease in the distress caused by your dynamic mind, work on observing, watching, and paying attention to what happens when you practice a skill.
- If you notice a shift in the distress that comes with your harsh thoughts, that's great – that's a bonus – but it's not the purpose of practicing unhooking skills.
- Defusion skills have nothing to do with proving or disproving thoughts but with the purpose of learning to watch them, have them, and see them for what they are: letters, words, sentences, and images that your dynamic mind gets busy with.

- Practicing unhooking skills is about getting better and better at having all different types of internal private experiences, especially the difficult ones and the ones that push you to act in ways that are incongruent with your personal values.

Now, let me take a mini-detour and briefly share some details from the autobiography of Andre Agassi, one of best tennis players in the world. I promise you that this side story is related to this chapter.

In his book, *Open*, Agassi (2010) wholeheartedly shares how much he hated tennis, how often he felt lonely, how he was unclear about what was important to him, how he progressively felt disconnected from the game as his career was unfolding, and how, despite enjoying international recognition and winning many tournaments, he often felt lost, unfulfilled, and like a failure. For Agassi, everything shifted – the contradiction between the life he was living and the life he wanted to have – when he realized that he had a choice on how to relate to tennis, what tennis could mean to him, and what he wanted to make of it (if you haven't read Agassi's biography, I highly, highly recommend it).

Going back to this chapter and unhooking skills, keep Andre Agassi's struggles in mind as you dive into the skills.

- *Name them and see them:*

    When your mind starts coming up with those judgmental, critical, and harsh thoughts that push you down into a rabbit hole of worry, fear, and anxiety, you can name them and imagine them as static or moving images of cartoons, characters, or objects.

    So, if Andre Agassi were to notice his internal narratives like, "I'm a failure", he could name the thought something like "the mess story" and then imagine it as the printed title of a book, the subject of an email, text on a webpage he found while surfing the Internet, printed letters on a cereal box, the name of a movie company, and so on.

    Agassi could also visualize those thoughts as cartoon characters, signs on taxis driving on the freeway, printed letters on the jerseys of baseball players running onto the field, words inside bubbles of air popping as they move up toward the sky, little ghosts moving in a haunted house – you get the idea.

- *Name them and say them:*

    You can also name your troublesome thoughts and say them quickly, slowly, aloud, quietly, or to yourself; you can scramble them, sing them, or say them in a silly voice or in the voice of a fictional character, such as Mickey Mouse, Ronald McDonald, or Homer Simpson.

    Going back to Agassi, he could bring into his mind his thoughts of being a failure, name these thoughts "the failure story", and say the thoughts fast for 30 seconds, repeat them in a humorous voice while pinching his nose, sing them to the tune of "Happy Birthday", say them backward ("e-ruy-laif-a-gni-eb"), scramble different versions of them as full words ("failure a being," "a being failure"), or scramble the syllables of the words ("afailurebeing," "urebeingafail," "failbeureing"), and so on.

- *Physicalizing them*:

    You can also give some physical characteristics to your troublesome thoughts by imagining them with a shape, color, size, interior texture, weight, speed, temperature, or exterior texture.

    To do this, Agassi could close his eyes for a moment and physicalize those self-loathing thoughts as an amorphous shape of flat dark-blue color, heavy and cold like ice cubes, with coarse texture on the outside, and a soft consistency on the inside. He could stay in this visualization for a couple of moments so he could make room for all the feelings that come along without running away from them.

None of these skills would make Andre Agassi's emotional pain go away when he was having harsh thoughts, but they would help him let go of the feeling of fighting, resisting, or wrestling with them, and keep him from letting those thoughts affect his behavior in a way that would take him far from his values.

Pause and Play

As silly as these defusion skills might sound, I strongly urge you to:

- Try them out.
- Choose the ones that you relate to most.
- Keep in mind why and how you're putting them into action.
- Watch your process with curious eyes.
- Let go of fighting against your feelings, and do your best to make room for them to come and go.

Playing the workability game means going beyond all the noise that your dynamic mind creates in order to understand and harness the unbelievable beauty and power of your high-achieving behaviors.

31 Mini-Me Stories

DOCTOR: Are you 5' 2"? (looks at me and my medical records, with a confused expression)
ME: Yes.
DOCTOR: I think you mean 5' .2" (looks at me with gentle but firm eyes).
ME: Really? (making a surprised face)
DOCTOR: Yup, you cannot be 5' 2". You're 5' . . . just 5' (in a flat tone of voice).
ME: What about the 2? (feeling a bit concerned)
DOCTOR: That's 0.2, not 2.
ME: I'm officially part of the "shorty" category.
DOCTOR: You have been part of the shorty category for a while, not just starting now.
ME: No comment.

I left the doctor's office with the official narrative that I was short. It wasn't new information; I kind of knew it. But there was something unique about that moment when the doctor looked at me, confused about the discrepancy between what he read and what he saw. I giggled softly as I walked through the hallway of the building toward my car, noticing how I had other narratives floating around in my brain: immigrant . . . psychologist . . . woman . . . working-class person . . . Latino . . . a person with an accent . . . strong . . . driven . . . caring . . . strict . . . lonely . . . selfish . . . not-good-enough.

Our relentless minds not only go into things wanting to do them precisely, efficiently, and as sharply as possible, but they also go into narrating mode.

Think about it: were there any silly stories that your mind came up with when you were a kid or a teenager? What about in your early twenties? Midthirties?

Here is one story my mind came up with. When I was a kid, I thought there were small people living inside the TV and radio, so I used to stand next to these devices and say, "Come on, little people, come out so I can see you. Let's play. I can put you inside my pockets and take you for a stroll in my bedroom."

These stories vary from silly, sassy, and goofy to tragic, sad, and upsetting – and everything in between. The fact is that no dynamic mind goes a day without coming up with narratives, stories, tales, or accounts of what happens to us, what occurs to others around us, and what happens to the world around us. And of course, our dynamic minds also come up with stories about who we are as people. Psychologists have referred to this particular content of our minds using terms like schema, core belief, self-concept, self-narrative, self-esteem, and many others; they all refer to the fact that we think deeply about ourselves.

Within ACT, we refer to this particular type of mind content as stories – strings of words and sentences – that our dynamic minds put together to make sense of our internal and external worlds. At the heart of our dynamic minds, there is an absolute imperative to understand the world within us and around us.

Some of these stories about who you are as a person are factual (e.g., I'm a woman. I'm an immigrant. I'm a psychologist). In Chapter 11, Personal Narratives, we briefly touched upon the fear of being a failure, not-good-enough, unlovable, or a mess. But what about other stories that your dynamic mind comes up with about who you are, whether they occur over and over or are new ones?

Are you willing to jot them down?

It's possible that when writing down these narratives, or even just thinking about them, you may feel some hesitation about committing them to paper. Some of these stories may feel so true to you; they may come with feelings of shame, embarrassment, guilt, sadness . . . and may even ask you to hide yourself to avoid making them real. You may have urges to talk back to these stories by listing all types of positive qualities you have, positive feedback you have received, and positive comments your friends have made about you as an evidence that you're not that story.

All those strategies make as much sense as any other thinking strategy you acknowledged in Chapter 22, The Great Escape, because they help you cope with the pain that comes from the stories; but they also give the stories much more power because you're still taking them as the absolute truth and relating to them as such.

Even if those narratives are justified, all those words together in the form of stories are not evidence that you're bad, broken, or defective. And, just to clarify, I'm not saying that you should quickly dismiss them or put up with them; I'm not saying that the pain caused by these stories isn't real or that it should be ignored. But I'm saying that of all those words, "not-good-enough" is one of the favorite stories that your mind comes up with and all the effort you put into reacting, proving wrong, or getting rid of them usually makes your life harder.

You can keep trying to argue back with those stories with positive thinking – as hundreds of people try – but many people have tried and failed because those stories keep coming back. You can also try to tell your mind to stop thinking badly about you, to stop coming up with stories, but that's another way of getting hooked and trying to get rid of those narratives.

The more you debate and fight any of those not-good-enough narratives, the stronger they become. Even though you may feel a tiny bit of relief from them, all the stories will come back, bigger and louder than before, and scream for your attention over and over. You're unlikely to win that debate with your dynamic mind because your mind is insistent and is always in content-generating mode.

The reality is that, as you continue working through this book – and I hope you will – and continue living, you are going to feel the push and pull between hiding from these narratives and reacting to them. But, luckily, there is another way to handle them that is a much more effective, long-lasting, and helpful way to deal with those narratives.

> ### Pause and Play
>
> Doing what works, doing things your way, and tapping into the benefits of high-achieving deeds means that you learn to experience all those stories for what they are: personal narratives. Like feelings, these personal narratives will rise and fall like waves if we let ourselves experience them without acting on them. So, every time your mind tells you that "you're not achieving, you're not an accomplished person, you're lazy, dumb or stupid," here is what you can do:
>
> - Take a deep, slow, and gentle breath.
> - Be curious about those stories: how do they look?
>
>   Are those stories coming in pictures or narratives? What type of voice do they come up with? How does the voice sound? What's the rhythm of the voice?
>
> - Name those stories in a way that helps you to step back from them.
>
>   You can choose any name you want. I choose "mini-me stories" for mine, but you can choose any name that helps you to recognize those stories when they come your way.
>
> - Take those stories for a walk with you.
>
>   As silly as it sounds, after naming your story, imagine how it looks and take it for a walk with you.

32 Terrible Feelings

Take stock: how many emotions do you experience from when you wake up in the morning until you fall asleep at night? What's your guess? Hundreds and hundreds, right?

Every moment you breathe and you're alive, you are also living an ongoing stream of emotions that comes and goes. This stream of emotions is not a fixed one but one in which your emotions shift in how you feel them, how long they last, and where you feel them in your body. Some emotions are on the fleeting side of this continuum and others land on the long-lasting side. Some emotions fluctuate between being pleasurable, comfortable, and fun, while others can be annoying, upsetting, and difficult. Some of your feelings swing between being localized, precise, and well-defined sensations to being mobile, dispersed, and scattered ones within your body.

But at the end of the day, this back-and-forth experience of your emotions is constant, and it requires that you work through them and with them so they don't end up defining what you say, think, or do.

In this chapter you're going to dive one more time into our wonderful emotions, but in particular the ones that come along with those not-good-enough stories that we discussed in the chapter Mini-Me Stories.

Think for a moment, if you scan back over those not-good-enough narratives that your mind screams at you, how do they feel in your body? Where do you feel them? What do you feel like doing when you think of them? Identifying those terrible feelings is important, because feelings lead to all types of actions, workable and unworkable ones.

This particular group of feelings can feel crushing, never-ending, and devastating. In my book *Escaping the Emotional Roller Coaster: ACT for the Emotionally Sensitive* (Zurita Ona, 2018), I describe these emotions as:

- Spreadable like butter: because you experience those stories and respective feelings in different areas of your life.
- Historical like an antique: because you have experienced them at different times in your life, not just now.
- Defiant like a wrestler: because they fight for survival.

- Painful like a sting: because they come with overwhelming amounts of pain.
- Deceitful like a con artist: because they trick you with that strong narrative about who you are, as if they really define you.

Once you learn to catch those stories and those feelings and stay with them, then you can make choices about how you want to respond to them; but if you push them too quickly, you will be lost in the land of the unpleasant stuff that comes with unchecked perfectionistic behaviors. And for the record, I'm not talking about feeling miserable with those feelings in a masochistic way; I'm talking about learning to make room for them as way of allowing yourself to feel the full range of human emotions.

> ### Pause and Play
>
> The skill of identifying our emotions is called emotional granularity and is linked with more effective behaviors and less problematic ones in all areas of our lives. You may be aware of some of your emotions but many times, our feelings move under the surface of our awareness, governing our actions. When you learn to recognize those terrible feelings that accompany those personal stories and stay with them, you develop a new relationship with your emotions, one that shapes your choices, your actions, and who you want to be.
>
> Here is a workable move you can make when those personal stories show up along with terrible feelings:
>
> - Watch them, label them, name them, tag them.
>
>   You may choose to observe your emotions as they feel in your body and without thinking of them.
>
> - Describe to yourself what you're feeling, sensing, and thinking as those experiences truly are:
>
>   Here is a thought of . . .
>   Here is a feeling of . . .
>   Here is a sensation of . . .
>
> These micro-skills may sound simplistic and even insignificant, but if you practice them, do it often, and are open to new things, you will notice how they help you to disentangle from those stories and all the pain that comes with them.
>
> Now, labeling your difficult emotions requires that you acknowledge them, and you can acknowledge them by saying . . .

33 Pleased to Meet You!

Let's face it, terrible feelings are hard to have, feel, and breathe through. But as you read in different chapters, instead of putting all your energy into fixing those annoying feelings, solving them, or blocking them, it is much more helpful to make room for them.

This skill of making room for the troublesome feelings that come your way – when making decisions, dealing with personal narratives, when criticizing yourself, and others – is called acceptance. You may have heard and read about acceptance in other contexts because, over the years, it has become a trendy word. So, just to be on the same page, let me clarify right away that acceptance is much more than just a nice, popular, or trendy word.

Within ACT, we think of acceptance as an active decision you make to sit with, take in, and open up to those crushing emotions that can take you away from being who you want to be, drag you in directions you don't need to go, or pull you into hours of rumination. But making space for those feelings has nothing to do with giving up or being a doormat to them. It's actually the opposite: accepting all types of painful emotions is actively, intentionally, and purposefully opening the door to them as they come, which is a very courageous thing to do!

What about doing a mini-exercise before continuing on with this chapter?

Find an index card or a sticky note and write down a feeling you struggle with – any feeling you want to focus on for this exercise is fine. Next, place that piece of paper between both of your hands – make sure it's between both palms – and press them against each other for a couple of moments, as hard as you can; notice how your arms and hands feel. Notice what it's like in your body. Then stop squeezing your hands but still hold the paper between them, noticing how it feels to be holding it without applying the pressure.

Did you notice the difference between pushing your hands against each other versus holding the paper without squeezing?

Squeezing the paper is like all the effort you put into blocking, suppressing, and trying to get rid of the annoying emotions that come with the stories about who you are, fears about not getting things right, worries about failing or anxiety about disappointing others. Think for

DOI: 10.4324/9781003083153-39

a moment, what happens when you push away those emotions as hard and fast as you can? How hard is it to engage in the things that matter to you when you're busy managing those feelings? Are you able to fully focus on what's in front of you?

Given that you don't have a control switch in your body to make these emotions disappear, are you open to trying something different? I cannot promise that any of those annoying feelings won't ever show up again when you care deeply about something, but I can tell you that learning to open up to them, without using any safety crutches, will take you very far in your goal of living a purposeful life.

Before you get cranky with me, keep in mind that I'm not asking you to love, like, or enjoy any those uncomfortable emotions and I'm not trying to minimize the struggle that comes with them. I know it's not easy to navigate through turbulent emotions. They hurt. And yet, they don't need to have power over you. Practicing acceptance as a life skill, and going back to it again and again, will help you to get better at making long-lasting, values-based choices and help you feel less stuck and make more workable moves!

Now, you can attempt to practice acceptance kicking and screaming and saying, "I hate this emotion! Why is this happening to me?" but that's not acceptance; it's judging the emotion and opening the door for rumination. Acceptance is about saying, "Here is shame," and if you want to take it further, you might say, "Shame, pleased to meet you."

Pause and Play

To up the workability game, you need to keep in mind that there is nothing to be solved or fixed when you're having difficult feelings, even though it may feel different.

When noticing a terrible feeling or troublesome emotion related to high-achieving behaviors:

- Imagine it as an object. Describe the shape, color, size, temperature, movement, and even weight of it. Describe it without judgment!
- You can use acceptance prompts, which are sweet, soft, and gentle ways to make room for all your feelings without fighting them.

When using an acceptance prompt, you can tell yourself things like: I want to do my best to watch this feeling coming and going, without pushing it away; I want to do the best I can to let this feeling come and go; I want to get through this feeling without becoming a puppet of it.

34 Plus and Minus

Having go-getting tendencies makes you susceptible to getting hooked onto stories about who you are, attaching strongly to them, and acting on them without being fully aware of it. You identified these stories in Chapter 11, Personal Narratives; in Chapter 31, Mini-Me Stories, we agreed that fighting them makes things worse for you, and that learning to take them for a walk will help you to have them without being directed by them.

These personal narratives can be so resistant to change because they're historical, have shifted, and, quite likely, have driven your actions many times. So, let's touch base about them one more time, but this time, let's touch base about all the mental calculations our minds do with these stories, as if our personal narratives are a math equation that needs to be solved.

Think about it: usually, the narratives our dynamic minds generate are a combination of positive and negative ones.

Positive narratives: I'm smart; I'm better than others; I'm clever; I'm detailed-oriented; I'm precise; I'm silly; I'm independent; I'm productive; I'm smart; I'm loyal; I'm reliable.

Negative narratives: I'm unworthy; I'm selfish; I'm damaged; I'm fake; I'm an impostor.

There are also the stories we tell ourselves that make our stomachs churn, and yet we relate to them over and over: I'm an alcoholic; I'm a workaholic; I'm needy; I'm selfish.

Take a moment to consider the three main stories your mind says about you and who you are:

I am ...
I am ...
I am ...

These repetitive and persistent stories may also push you to feel unworthy, ashamed, or undeserving. You may have a strong urge to keep doing everything right and perfectly so those stories don't reveal themselves.

We all have a narrative – or many of them – about who we are. Our narratives are complex and multidimensional, and include many things we've decided about ourselves based on our experiences, learnings, hopes, dreams, aspirations, and misfortunes. And as our minds are constantly generating content, the list of narratives keeps growing.

Russ struggled to show up on time to his daughter's rehearsal, so his mind quickly went to the narrative: I'm an inconsiderate father; I'm fake. I preach about showing up for my kids, and here I am, failing my daughter.

Are we those stories?

Are we defined by those narratives?

Are those stories about ourselves factual?

The most popular solution to solve the problem of our stories was to add positive ones and subtract negative ones. In fact, thousands of books on self-esteem have been written within that frame with the purpose of increasing it as much as possible. But, this approach has not demonstrated any benefits; in fact, forcing positive narratives about ourselves has been linked to ineffective individualistic actions, low cooperation with others, and a tendency to avoid activities that could threaten one's self-concept (Baumeister, Campbell, Krueger, & Vohs, 2003; Mueller & Dweck, 1998). Quite shocking findings, right?

Side comment: now you're getting a sense of why and how passionate I am about behavioral science. Behavioral science goes beyond popular knowledge, deconstructs it, questions it, and reconstructs it again; without behavioral science, we'll be at the mercy of living our lives under false premises that could actually hurt us (if you're interested in what's new in behaviorism, I wrote a blog post here: www.thisisdoctorz.com/the-old-the-new-whats-in-about-being-a-behaviorist/).

Going back to the self-esteem problem...

The fact is that you can't prevent your mind or my mind from coming up with negative stories, eliminate those painful feelings that come along, or control all the experiences we go through so we don't feel bad about ourselves. We do feel imperfect so many times. And here is another important fact: no self-esteem book, program, boot camp, or therapy program has the power to eliminate your narratives forever.

The narrative that you are worthy is hard to create by making lists of your positive virtues or hoping for good feelings to come your way or waiting for the right circumstances to happen. Improving your so-called self-esteem cannot be done by looking at it as a math formula that needs to equal positive stories or positive feelings.

The narrative of who you really are can only be found in your actions, the choices you make, self-acceptance, and your willingness to face the inner struggle of your mind.

Pause and Play

You cannot keep your dynamic mind from generating stories about who you are; as long as you're alive, that's how it's going to be.

Here are micro-skills you can apply when having those personal stories:

- Picture for a moment that your mind is a politician, knocking door-to-door, soliciting your vote. This particular politician is asking you to go along with annoying stories of not being good enough, asking you to imagine all types of negative things. This politician has called you, texted you, and come to your front door, all to push your buttons. This politician knows what to tell you, how to grab your attention, and how to push you.

    But this time you decide how to respond to this politician in your mind. You can fight back, argue, try to reason, go along with the ideas, or ignore the politician completely. You can also ask yourself: what's the most effective move I can make in those moments of hurt when my mind is in politician mode pulling me in different directions?

35 Don't Go Down the Rabbit Hole!

> An adult man in his midthirties walks slowly toward a microphone. He stands stoically and opens his mouth; his face makes the movements of someone talking, and yet no words are coming out, only guttural sounds – followed by loooong awkward silence.

Have you watched the movie *The King's Speech*? If not, I super-encourage you to do so – of course, only if you're into watching movies, as I am (as you know by now).

In this film, Geoffrey Rush and Colin Firth do amazing jobs acting as, respectively, a psychologist and the future King George VI of England, the latter of whom struggles with a fear of public speaking born of stuttering.

George VI is scared of talking in front of others. He stutters most when feeling anxious, when having to give speeches, when having to speak into a microphone, or when giving an interview in front of a large crowd.

Let's think for a moment of Richard. Richard, a gay Jewish man, was ready to be in a committed romantic relationship; he really wanted to start a family, connect with a partner, and grow old together. So, he didn't think twice about enrolling in a Jewish dating service for the gay community. After carefully crafting his profile, with details from his life represented in different pictures, he started exchanging texts and having phone conversations with potential partners. When catching up with his friends, he shared that some of the people he had been interacting with were smokers, others were too fat, others ate pork regularly, others were vegan, others were too short, others were too tall, others loved to party too much, others seemed too religious, others were not smart enough, others were not financially stable, and others were too nerdy.

Back in his apartment, sitting in front of his laptop, Richard started questioning himself, "What if I don't ever find my person? What if I made a mistake breaking up with my ex? Will I die alone, old, and bald? Will I ever have a family of my own? What if I fall down in my apartment, get a concussion, and there is nobody to help?" That night, Richard tried to fall asleep, but his mind kept coming back at him with thoughts of him being broken, unlovable, and a loser. He got busy entertaining all those

DOI: 10.4324/9781003083153-41

possibilities and scenarios, one after another. He ended up feeling bad about himself, hopeless, and despite his eagerness to connect with potential partners, he didn't schedule any dates that month.

It's a reality that when something matters to you, you may get concerned about messing it up for yourself and others, as George VI in the movie or Richard. All your fears, worries, and anxieties get amplified, maximized, and elevated to a level that, if you don't pay attention, you end up in a rabbit hole.

Richard took those worries as facts and engaged with them as any reasonable person – who didn't read this book – will do. Is it wrong that Richard was worried about finding the partner of his dreams? Not necessarily. But what he's missing are two micro-skills: (1) differentiating when going into a rabbit hole is helpful and when it isn't and (2) connecting with the values behind his worries (Richard was missing that, behind all his worries, he was afraid of choosing the wrong partner; he was afraid of ending up with an imperfect partner).

> **Pause and Play**
>
> Worries are creations of our dynamic minds and not necessarily thoughts to dwell on over and over all the time. I don't think you want to spend your life as a dedicated, dutiful, and committed worrier, right?
>
> Next time you find your mind is attempting to take you into a rabbit hole, ask yourself these questions:
>
> - What happens if I don't worry about [insert the topic you're worrying about]?
> - How would I feel about myself if I didn't worry about [insert the topic you're worrying about]?
> - What's the value behind my worries?
>
> Remember that the first worry thought is on your mind, but going down a rabbit hole is on you.

36 Daring to Be Kind!

As Milan was completing the online forms for her graduate school applications, she took a deep breath and noticed how hectic, fast, and overwhelming the process had been. She sipped her tea and remembered how hard she had studied in middle school, how many extra college-level classes she had taken to raise her grades, how many gatherings she had declined attending so she wouldn't be tired for a test the following day, how many silent tears had stung her face, how many thousands of hours she'd researched in the library of her college, all so she could earn good grades. Milan also thought about how scary it was that she had worked so hard but could still potentially mess up this application and ruin her opportunity to go to a prestigious grad school. Milan's mind was reeling as she continued to fill out the forms. She noticed a strong sensation in her chest, a familiar feeling, and she noticed how scared she was about failing, about not succeeding, about not fulfilling her dreams. She thought to herself, "I'm just an imposter, a failure of a person in the end." Then, she had thoughts about being an idiot for not working harder to prepare. She thought she was an irresponsible person for going out to dinner the weekend before, instead of researching more college programs; she was lazy for not making the time to write drafts of her essays months ago. In these moments, she felt lonely and disconnected from what was in front of her. She started to cry. This is not what Milan had expected to happen today since she had woken up very early with only one agenda in mind: to submit four applications.

Imagine that you met Milan in a moment like this: what would you tell her?

Milan was getting hooked on a narrative that her dynamic mind came up with. Our minds, in addition to doing their best to protect us, are also problem-solving machines and try to make sense of what has gone wrong, what happened, our disappointments, and our frustrations, all at one time. As a result, we sometimes end up with a narrative that sounds like evidence of how defective we are! That's exactly what Milan was experiencing. She got fused with a narrative about failing, not succeeding, not fulfilling her dreams, and felt those familiar feelings that have been present many times in her life.

DOI: 10.4324/9781003083153-42

Daring to Be Kind! 121

Our minds move quickly to constructing coherent arguments about whatever our struggle is at the moment, but they don't always get it right! When we're hurting, our dynamic minds do their best to connect the dots, explain our suffering, and come up with a rational account of what happened.

What do you do when your dynamic mind comes up with a narrative that inundates you with self-criticizing thoughts, future stories, or worries about failing, as you are going about your day as usual? What did you do last month when your mind decided to list all your imperfections, limitations, and flaws as you were moving through your day?

You may be tempted to handle that pain by rationalizing and convincing yourself of your good character, talents, and successes; you may be urged to get confirmation from others that you're not broken, that you're worthy. If you do question your mind, what happens when you wrestle with all of the rationalizing responses? How long does it last, this wrestling with your mind? For how long are you able to convince yourself of your worth until the old narratives come back?

You may also be tempted to push down these emotions – to pretend they're not there and keep going. You may try hard to think of something positive or to bring into your mind a happy memory so you can feel better. You may try to distract from the feelings by shopping, using substances, or seeking more pleasurable experiences.

If you do engage in any of these behaviors, or variations on them, how long does it take for the painful feelings to show up again?

One way to handle those moments of hurt is self-compassion. Self-compassion cannot be given to us; it's not a book that someone can hand to us or something that someone else can practice for us.

I like to think of self-compassion as a kind, gentle, and caring response to ourselves – and also as a decision we make to handle those hurtful moments by actively caring for ourselves.

It's possible that your dynamic mind may argue back with thoughts like, "How can you be kind when you don't feel good about yourself? How can you be kind with yourself if you don't believe you're worthy?"

If so, keep these important considerations in mind:

- Feeling good about yourself and believing you're worthy are not prerequisites to being kind to yourself.
- If you wait to feel good about yourself before being kind to yourself, you could wait a lifetime.
- If you wait to believe you're worthy before being kind to yourself, you could wait a lifetime too.

Pause and Play

As your day unfolds and different types of self-criticizing stories or hurtful moments show up, you can put into action some of these micro-skills:

- Ask yourself, "how can I show kindness to myself in this moment?"

    (Some suggestions: you could write a caring letter to yourself; you could remind yourself that you're giving your best; you could give yourself a break; you can show empathy toward yourself)
- Acknowledge that you're hurting by telling yourself things like, "I'm struggling right now. This hurts. This feels painful."
- Acknowledge that your dynamic mind is coming up with a coherence narrative, and give it a name – don't judge or criticize it, don't fight it, don't rationalize it, just let it be.
- Coach yourself as you would coach any other person if you were witnessing their pain.

Going back to Milan for a moment, what would you have told her? If you were to write her a note, what would it say?

Here is what my note would say: I'm sorry you're going through this; I know you worked so hard for years to reach your dreams. I know that you put a lot of work into getting good grades, doing extra things, and always doing your best on everything you could have done to secure your career path. I'm sorry that, right now, your mind is telling you all this stuff that makes you doubt yourself, your career, your future. What can I do to help?

Daring to be kind is a much more workable move in the long term.

37 Vulnerabilities or Liabilities?

In one of my years training as a psychologist, I delivered therapy/coaching services in an elementary school.

On a Tuesday morning, I received a call from a teacher about an eight-year-old student who had been crying for the last hour and was being sent to my office. I went to find him in the hallway and saw him sobbing as he walked slowly – red eyes, tears running down his cheeks, deeply distressed.

After introducing myself, I walked with him the rest of the way to my office, and we both sat down; his crying continued. No words could stop his tears, and it wasn't helpful to force him to talk. Waiting patiently as he sipped a glass of water was a helpful move in that moment. He lifted his head, looked around the room, and said, "I failed … " as his eyes got to watering again.

I gently asked more and learned that he'd taken a math test a week ago, had gotten the results this morning, and had missed two questions. When talking to the teacher, I learned that this wasn't the first time he'd been extremely disappointed by his performance. When I talked to his mom, she agreed with the teacher's impression and added that he often gets upset with his sister when she doesn't follow game rules; he demands that she respect them and cries inconsolably at times.

How is it for you when you make mistakes and errors when things matter profoundly to you?

Every human being makes mistakes, gets things wrong, and has slip-ups; that's just human nature. But when you care deeply about something and have high-achieving and perfectionistic tendencies, navigating mistakes can be hard, really hard, and terribly hard. It's like, in those moments, your dynamic mind gets hooked on thoughts like *Making a mistake means I'm a failure. I should have prevented this. I should have known better. What's wrong with me? Am I an idiot?* And these thoughts are quickly followed by battering yourself with criticism, shame, and negative judgments.

Atelophobia, the fear of making mistakes, is a real thing.

Perhaps it is discouraging for you that when one thing goes wrong, everything feels less than acceptable. Maybe it is painful to see how your dynamic mind cannot stop criticizing you when a mistake happens.

DOI: 10.4324/9781003083153-43

Possibly it's confusing that, despite working harder than most people and always giving your best, you feel as if you're not-good-enough, worthy, or lovable. Perhaps it's distressing that when you look around, so many things look good in your life, and yet, a particular mistake feels like it eliminates all that goodness. Maybe seeing or hearing that something you did is less than perfect feels like your heart is being ripped out.

It's hard to face our mistakes. But it's harder when your mind perceives any errors you make as liabilities that have to be managed in order to keep your worth, identity, and abilities from being compromised. It's definitely harder when you tend to demand a lot from yourself. And it's much harder to manage setbacks when your nature is to push yourself to overachieve in the things you do.

The truth is that, despite our best efforts, we make mistakes of all types, sizes, and colors – missing an appointment, forgetting to pay a bill, saying the wrong thing, forgetting to take the cake out of the oven, losing our patience with someone, not practicing enough before an important competition, and on and on. There are, of course, mistakes that have significant implications. And yet, most of the things we do wrong do not prove to be fatal.

I'm not saying that it's okay to make a mistake. I'm not saying that you should relax after dropping the ball. And I'm not saying that you should just move on after making an error. I'm saying that it's important for you to check how you respond to your mind screaming at you when you've caught an error, creating a sense of urgency for you, and repeatedly telling you that an error diminishes your worth.

Does engaging in those thoughts get you to do more in your life, or does it take you into hours of self-criticism, shame, and disappointment? Check for yourself.

I can honestly tell you that there is a very, very, very thin line between treating yourself with tough love and going into a spiral of self-deprecation (you will read more about this in Chapter 45).

For now, I would like to invite you to consider that, at the end of the day, your imperfections, flaws, and failings could be an essential part of your life; they may not necessarily be proof of your character, but rather serve as proof of our common humanity.

Perhaps your fumbles could teach you how to continue loving yourself, how to fully and wholeheartedly accept yourself, and how much you care about the things you participate in.

Pause and Play

When an unfortunate mistake happens, instead of reacting, assuming, and jumping into harsh criticisms:

- Thank your mind for trying to protect you from making that mistake in the future. You can literally say to yourself, *Thanks, mind! I get that you're working hard to make sure I'm okay in the future; I get it.*

- Go back to Chapter 30, Minding and Unwinding, and choose one of the defusing skills to help you handle the difficult thoughts.
- Go back to Chapter 33, Pleased to Meet You!, and do your best to observe your feelings as they come and go.

38 Less Chasing, More Choosing

THE MODEL: What are you doing?
THE PAINTER: Sometimes, you know, you can only do something by undoing it.
THE MODEL: Yes, but how many times?
THE PAINTER: That's a good question.
THE MODEL: What is it?
THE PAINTER: The undoing of something.
THE MODEL: I thought the portrait looked really good earlier, when we started.
THE PAINTER: It can be very easy and very tempting to be satisfied with what's easy, when people tell you something is good. There, that's good. But...

In the film *Final Portrait*, Alberto Giacometti, a famous Swiss artist played by Geoffrey Rush, offers to paint a portrait of his friend James Lord, an American writer. While the portrait starts as an afternoon project, it ends up in 19 days of delay, the cancellation of multiple trips to New York, and the deepening of Giacometti and Lord's friendship. It also gives us an insight into Giacometti's tense pursuit of the perfect portrait.

Giacometti comes close to finishing the portrait multiple times but is driven by an exquisite attentiveness to its different elements. When he sees a detail that feels off or that doesn't look right, he paints over the portrait, covering it with a layer of black paint and then a layer of white paint. He screams, "It's not ready! It's mediocre!" Giacometti and Lord spend many afternoons repeating their routine: Lord sitting down in an old chair, doing his best to remain still in the same posture, and chatting about random subjects; Giacometti switching between looking at Lord and painting on the canvas. Some afternoons, they only spend an hour in the studio, and others, four to five hours. But most afternoons, Giacometti, full of frustration, finishes their session abruptly and moves quickly to cover the portrait with black and then white paint.

Lord starts fearing Giacometti won't ever finish the portrait. He decides that his only chance to have this project see completion is to catch Giacometti at the precise moment when he's reaching for the

DOI: 10.4324/9781003083153-44

brush to paint over the portrait and distract him with a conversation about any random topic.

In some ways, Giacometti represents the agony, despair, and frustration that you may experience when things are not ready, when you haven't figured everything out, or when you haven't explored all the possibilities before making a decision. Giacometti's actions speak about your push to do more, to work hard, to triple-consider a decision before making a move. He represents the part of you that chases a feeling – that aha-feeling – that only comes when things are close to being perfectly done.

Is that chase familiar to you?

Elliot gets excited when his clothes fit him snugly, which means his weight is still between 180 and 200 pounds. Maurice smiles deeply after correctly playing every single note on his piano, without changing the cadence or adding pauses. Dave's heart gets to beating quickly when he's preparing the perfect meal for his partner.

How is it for you, wrestling with that push and pull in order to feel that aha-feeling? Do you avoid starting things unless you're sure you can see them through perfectly? Do you wait until conditions are perfect to go after what you want?

It's understandable that your dynamic mind would say, *It's not ready. I need more time. It's not there yet. I need to do it again*. It makes sense that you would often decide to postpone, procrastinate on, and delay a situation, task, or project. It's reasonable that you would chase those aha-feelings when you have clarity on what you're hoping to accomplish.

Within ACT, we call that particular pursuit of an aha-feeling an *emotional goal* because you're trying to control how you feel and hoping to feel a particular way. It's like you're chasing a feeling – but not just any feeling, the perfect feeling – as a prerequisite to getting things done or moving on to what's next.

Lukas is searching for a partner. When he goes on dates, he often dismisses a person because he's waiting for that aha-feeling – the perfect combination of attraction, connection, and excitement. Meanwhile, tons of research has shown that having that "strong feeling," like a waterfall or heavy metal music, is not a positive indicator of a long-lasting, committed, and fulfilling relationship.

If I were to ask Lukas, "How does it really feel when you don't experience that perfect feeling of attraction?" he might say, "I feel sad at not finding a partner, afraid that something is wrong with me, and embarrassed that all of my friends have a partner and I'm the only single person in the group."

What if, for Lukas to find the partner he needs, he must learn to sit with those feelings that he's pushing away instead of rushing to chase the aha-feeling? What if Lukas's relentless pursuit of that feeling of excitement is actually tricking him into chasing an emotional goal – a fleeting feeling that evaporates quickly?

Lukas may say, "But that aha-feeling is an important one, and it's an indication that I'm on the right track." An aha-feeling feels really good; it's like a strong rush of satisfaction, joy, and contentment! It's like getting high! And, as I would say as a hard-core behaviorist, it's appetitive (an experience you want to have more and more of). So, of course, you might struggle to let it go.

Lukas remembered how it felt to have those exciting feelings – like butterflies in his stomach – when meeting someone and going out the first few times; he also remembered how disappointing it was to not have those feelings as he was getting to know a potential partner. He often took the lack of those feelings as an indicator that the relationship wasn't going to work, that a person was not a good partner for him, or that the relationship wasn't a good fit – and, quickly, he would move on.

I'm not suggesting that it's okay to do sloppy work, carelessly complete a task, or speak uncaringly to others. I'm saying that every moment you spend searching for those aha-feelings and treating them as prerequisites to doing what matters, going after the stuff you care about, and moving forward with important things, you are also pursuing a road to suffering.

Pause and Play

Happiness, joy, and contentment come with knowing we're doing things that are important to us with great care. And even though these feelings are transitory, there is long-lasting happiness that can come from the choices we make every day of our lives.

So, every time you find yourself chasing that aha-feeling, take a deep breath, acknowledge the push to keep searching for it, and ask yourself:

- What is my chase in service of?
- What is the chase protecting me from?
- What is my mind protecting me from facing?
- Am I committed to chasing a feeling or to having a fulfilling life?
- How is this chase working in my life as a whole?

39 When-Then Thoughts

Samir, a well-known lawyer, was having dinner with his 72-year-old father. After tasting a rich, full-bodied, and sweet Cabernet, his father said, in a firm tone of voice, "Samir, when are you going to expand your law firm?"

Samir looked his father in the eyes, and then, looking down, saw for the first time his truth. "Dad, when I was five, you told me to play piano so I could develop an artistic mind. In middle school, you told me to study hard so I could take college-level classes in high school. When I was in high school, you told me that I should go to law school. When I was in law school, you told me to practice medical law so I wouldn't have to worry about my financial future. When I became a medical lawyer, you told me that I should work privately instead of working at a company."

Samir realized in that moment how he had organized his life around his father's prescriptions, and how, for many years, he had been hooked on thoughts like *When I do this, then I'll be accepted by my father*.

In this chapter, we are going to take a look at another way in which these stories could be leading you to unworkable actions out of your awareness.

The walls of my office have heard many variations of statements like these:

- When I stop feeling anxious, then I'll be more myself.
- When I put my work out there, then I'll feel recognized.
- When my company is stable, then I will feel at peace.
- When I finish this project, then I'll feel more accomplished.
- When I see my kids graduating, then I will feel that I was a good parent.
- When I lose 25 pounds, then I'll be more comfortable with myself.
- When I find the right partner, then I'll be fulfilled.
- When I choose my college, then I'll be relaxed.

What are the when-then thoughts your mind holds onto?

I'm willing to bet that, as a person who gives your best in the things you do, each one of your when-then thoughts pushes you to do something (e.g., buy new electronics to be sure you have the best equipment

DOI: 10.4324/9781003083153-45

for your project; work extra hours so others will recognize your work; triple-check your work so your reputation is not compromised; count your calories so you can reach an ideal weight and appearance; avoid conflict and confrontation to make sure you're liked by others). These thoughts function similarly to the ruling-thoughts you read about in Chapter 10, Mental Rubrics, because they demand you do something almost habitually.

But let's step back and think for a moment: what are other potential reasons behind each one of those actions? What would happen if you didn't follow through with those when-then thoughts? How does it feel when you go along with them and do what they tell you to do?

While all the actions that accompany those when-then thoughts are reasonable steps you take, some of them may be strategies for managing the feelings and stories of not being good enough that you reflected on in different chapters in this book, such as Chapter 31, Mini-Me Stories, Chapter 11, Personal Narratives, and others.

Sometimes, no matter how much you have accomplished, no matter how much success you've experienced, no matter how much your friends love you, no matter how much your career has grown, and no matter what actions you take, there is still that feeling that you are not-good-enough. It's like no matter what you do that feeling and that story are always there, waiting to get your attention.

But engaging in actions driven by when-then thoughts will only make things much worse for you in the long term. Here's why:

Dealing with a not-good-enough story about yourself and wrestling with the feelings that come with it hurts. That's called primary pain. When you do all the unworkable stuff to manage those emotions and make them go away – instead of making room for them, accepting them, and showing yourself compassion – you're left with a second wave of hurt as a result of using those ineffective strategies. That's called secondary pain.

Going back to Samir, it's already painful for him to feel as if he's not-good-enough, not worthy, or not loved by his father just for being himself (primary pain). But when he gets hooked onto when-then thoughts and does one thing after another to try to handle those feelings of not being good enough – playing piano, taking college-level classes in high school, going to law school, becoming a medical lawyer – he feels frustrated, angry, and disappointed in himself for the life he has created (secondary pain).

You may be hoping that, one day, you will find the ultimate strategy for feeling good about yourself forever, but no one in the history of humanity has experienced that long-lasting feeling – and quite likely, no one ever will because it's not in our makeup. We can try very hard to always feel good about ourselves by buying more things, pleasing others more, drinking our favorite beers, or traveling to exotic places, but none of our nice feelings about ourselves will last forever. It's not your fault that you hunt those positive feelings or do everything you can to get rid of negative stories or get hooked on what-then thoughts. We all do. It's just that you're more prone to wrestling with those stories and emotions about yourself because you care deeply about doing things right in your life and being true to yourself. And up to this point, you have been managing all those internal experiences using all the tools you have at your reach.

Imagine for a moment that you have fallen into a hole. Down there, all you have with you are the painful feelings that come with the not-good-enough narrative and a shovel. You start digging and digging, trying to get out of the hole using the single shovel you have. The problem is that the more you dig with that familiar shovel, the deeper you get. This is how it is with you and all the things you're compelled to do by your when-then thoughts. You think you're managing the pain, but you're digging yourself deeper.

> **Pause and Play**
>
> The key to taking advantage of high-achieving tendencies is to catch those when-then thoughts as they occur, recognize the actions that come with them, and check their workability, ACT style.
>
> - Make a list of all the when-then thoughts your mind comes up with.
> - Check how your when-then thoughts influence your life: in your relationships with others and with yourself, in your career, and in other areas.
> - Ask yourself, *What are the feelings and stories I'm avoiding by going along with the when-then thoughts?*
> - Go back to Chapter 33, Pleased to Meet You!, Chapter 31, Mini-Me Stories, and Chapter 38, Less Chasing, More Choosing, to practice skills, name the themes of those narratives, and practice turning toward them.

40 Tough Choices Need Kindness

On a Wednesday afternoon in the middle of a warm spring, I was lying down on the couch in my living room, holding a packet of ice to my forehead. I had an awful migraine and an extraordinary sense of exhaustion that I hadn't felt in years. I thought it was stress; I thought I didn't sleep well that day; I thought maybe it was allergies. But the reality is that slowly and progressively my body had been feeling more and more tired; that day, I felt something like a switch turn off inside me; I went from having the energy to do the usual things I do to experiencing an awful sense of exhaustion.

After multiple medical tests over a couple of weeks, I learned that I had a significant iron deficiency – and when I say significant, I mean truly significant. My iron levels were so low that I was dragging my feet to take care of the things I needed to do during the day and going to bed between seven and eight o'clock most evenings. On top of that, despite taking daily iron supplements, I started having regular shortness of breath, as if I were close to having a panic attack. Thank goodness for my training: I knew that it was important to watch that wave come and go. Low levels of iron affect the levels of oxygen that go into your blood.

I deeply missed my bubbly energy, exercising, moving, and feeling like myself. For more than a year, I had to readjust every single thing I did because my body couldn't function. I could only maintain my energy levels for four to five hours at a time, and then I needed to rest for an hour or two in order to be able to do what I needed to do for another two to three hours, maximum. My days shrunk to eight functioning hours or less, for everything: cooking, hanging out with people, cleaning, seeing clients, making phone calls, writing, exercising, and so on. On days when I felt okay and did a bit more for a bit longer, I felt fatigued for a few days after. It was a high price to pay.

The reality was brutal: I had to carefully choose where to allocate my eight hours of daily energy. I couldn't continue writing a manuscript I was working on. I couldn't continue preparing the online class I was developing. I couldn't exercise with the frequency I wanted. I couldn't hang out with people as much as I wanted.

It was a tough time. What was tough was that every moment I had to make a tough choice between things that I cared deeply about – my

DOI: 10.4324/9781003083153-46

relationships, my career, my personal growth, my health – the things I needed to do, and the regular things we all do on a daily basis.

Choosing between the things you care about is tough, but giving yourself the freedom to do so is liberating.

I got invited to do different presentations, to take long hikes, to contribute to writing projects, to spend a day at the beach, to conduct podcast interviews, and to go on weekend trips. With every invitation, I had to decide: do I choose to do this today?

With every choice, there was a sense of grief; saying yes to something that mattered meant saying no to something that mattered as well. With every choice, there were fears of coming across as rude, being annoying, missing career opportunities, or losing close friendships.

My body remembers still how all those months felt and how, with each tough choice, I danced with my fears.

What are the tough choices you've had to make?

How did you handle them?

I don't know how it was for you, but I can tell you that, for me, after making these daily choices and sensing my own fears, treating myself with kindness was a much needed and helpful move.

The reality is that none of the gatherings, invitations, or career opportunities I had to turn down will be back. They are gone.

I care for my friendships as much as I care for opportunities to disseminate behavioral science, create new resources for anyone struggling with fear-based reactions, or reflect on how I'm living my life. But living our values is not a path to power through toughening up or doing perfectly the things that matter to us. Living our values involves making choices, sometimes tough ones; we might have to walk away from something we care deeply about.

Pause and Play

I would like to invite you to:

- Give yourself permission to make tough choices and walk away from some things that you care about instead of trying to do it all.
- Give yourself a gentle touch of kindness, compassion, and caring after each tough choice you make – as if someone that cares about you were giving you a hug (in Chapter 36, Daring to Be Kind!, you read about kindness practices).

Section VI

Onward and Upward!

So, here we are in the last section of this book! What a journey it's been to write this book; I hope that reading it has been a good experience for you!

In everyday language, ACT aims to help you build a rich, meaningful, and fulfilling life. It does this by helping you to: (a) clarify your values and use them to guide your actions; (b) learn psychological skills to develop a new relationship with your thoughts, feelings, and emotions; and (c) focus on what works and develop a new sense of vitality.

The word *vitality* comes from the Latin "vita," and it refers to life, drive, and passion. To be fully alive, present, and engaged with what matters requires that you learn to face the internal struggles you encounter as a person who cares deeply and is prone to working harder than others, doing the right thing at all times, feeling responsible for others, and continuously striving for the best possible outcomes.

We face all types of challenges, even when we're doing our best. In this section, we'll take a look at the micro-skills you need to nurture high-achieving and perfectionistic actions as our unpredictable, uncertain, and imperfect lives unfold. You will learn micro-skills to break free from the shackles of perfectionism that keep you stuck, do more of what works, and build a life of freedom, fulfillment, and vitality.

Enjoy this last section!

41 Messy Moments

Let me start this chapter by asking you some questions:

- Were there any dishes you ate last month that you didn't like?
- Did you receive any unexpected bills that caught you by surprise?
- Did anyone frustrate you this month?
- Are there times when your mind takes you back to past situations that you wish you had handled differently?
- Have you found yourself dwelling on how you've disappointed others even when you didn't mean to?

How often do we have a day when things don't go south in some shape or form?

And as the popular saying goes, when it rains, it pours. At times, it's one thing after another, disaster after disaster, disappointment after disappointment, and sometimes even tragedy after tragedy.

Imagine how it would be if everything around us functioned in an absolutely perfect way: no one bumps you with their cart at the grocery store; your neighbors park their car in their own spot; your partner knows when to offer support and when to go into problem-solving mode; your parents get you.

Wouldn't it be amazing if things went as planned and as we wanted? And yet, as much as we may crave things going smoothly all the time, that's just fantasy.

If we looked at our lives and the lives of those around us, we'd see a collection of unforeseen situations happening to all of us – from the random ones, like our computers breaking down or having to wait longer than an hour for a doctor's appointment, to feeling the loss of people we love or feeling disappointed by the person we love.

In the midst of writing this manuscript, I received texts with news about three friends unexpectedly passing away, a friend losing her husband after a minor outpatient procedure, a friend losing herself to depression.... all those messages felt like a bucket of cold water.

As much as we try to minimize things going wrong, in the game of life, odds are that something will go wrong, terribly wrong. I don't mean to be pessimistic or radically realistic, but I do want to invite you to ponder

DOI: 10.4324/9781003083153-48

what happens when you do every single thing you can for things to go smoothly, straight, and as close to perfectly as possible, and then, despite your best efforts, something goes completely wrong. How do you handle those moments?

Grab a piece of paper, hold it between both hands, and bring it all the way up to your face, to where it's touching your nose. Imagine for a moment that the piece of paper represents what you have control over, what you can plan, what you can predict. Next, bring the paper down to your lap and notice the room around you.... The room represents the many things you don't have control over.

So, the big questions for you are, how do you do the things you care about when only some things are under your control and many more things are not? How do you keep doing the things that matter to you even when your mind holds on to "wishful thoughts" about people changing, things going in the right direction, or trying to keep bad things from happening?

A crucial micro-skill is to distinguish between what's really under your control (your responses to your thoughts, urges, emotions, feelings) and what's really not (other people's behaviors, unexpected things happening, technological mishaps, etc.).

Many years ago, in one of the rotations of my post-doctoral training, I met a young woman in her early twenties, let's name her Fibi. Fibi had been living with cystic fibrosis – a genetic and fatal disease that causes chronic lung infections – almost all her life. She tried all types of procedures to manage this disease – oxygen therapy, liver transplant, nasal surgery, feeding tube – but her body didn't respond positively and she knew that she did not have much longer to live. Fibi didn't have control of her illness and what it was doing to her body, but she chose to spend her remaining time celebrating the relationships with her family and the friends she met along the way.

> ### Pause and Play
>
> If you find yourself holding onto wishful thoughts about how things should be, how others should behave, how you should behave, or how things should be in the world, try these:
>
> - Check what you have control of and what you don't.
> - Check what happens when you keep holding onto any type of wishful thoughts.
> - Check how you feel when holding onto those wishful thoughts.
> - Ask yourself, "Is it effective to hold onto these wishful thoughts because things didn't go as I wanted?"
>
>   If the answer is no, go back to your values and from that place of caring ask yourself: what's one thing you could do to get closer to what's important in this moment of "stuckness"?

42 Living With Not Knowing

If I'd had a long day and wanted to relax by watching *Jane the Virgin*, it would make sense that, after pressing the "On" button on the TV's remote control, I would see a signal on the screen showing that the TV is on. But what happens if, after pressing the button, the screen remains off and I don't see anything?

I may quickly begin to wonder, "Is something wrong with the TV? Is the outlet working? Is the cable functioning properly?" There could be so many things causing the TV not to work. Naturally, I would feel confused because of the discrepancy between what I was expecting to happen – watching TV after pressing the "On" button – and what happened – watching the TV screen remain off after pressing the "On" button.

These unknown situations are not infrequent; in fact, it's the opposite. Every day of our lives, from the moment we wake up to the moment we go to sleep, there are many moments in which we have little information about what's going to happen or there is a mismatch between what we encounter and how we think it should be. For instance, if you open your laptop and it doesn't turn on, that's a nonsensical situation that your brain will quickly try to solve by running different scenarios: is the battery dead? Is something malfunctioning within the laptop? Did I press the power button hard enough?

Our minds spontaneously have a strong need to make sense of the nonsense, unknowns, and conflicts that show up. This urge to solve the unknown is not necessarily a bad thing; it's quite an adaptive response. In fact, without it, we wouldn't get anything done. Imagine that you're writing the end of a novel, helping your kid with schoolwork about a topic you're not familiar with, or discussing with your partner a potential job opportunity; in all these situations, managing ambiguity effectively will lead you to consider more options for the end of your novel, research relevant information to help your kid with school homework, and consider all options about the potential job before committing to a decision.

So, when we feel uncertain about any situation, we also experience a sense of urgency to solve it and we take action to solve it: we may search for more information, dismiss what we don't know, hold on with white knuckles to old beliefs, or make decisions to minimize the

DOI: 10.4324/9781003083153-49

unknown. Even when the unknown situation is good news (e.g., when you expect to be fired but your boss just wants to tell you about a new project), your mind still flies into action to solve that not-knowing situation.

> Sunil had been seeing Babak for over a year; they had traveled together, worked on house projects together, cooked together, and spent holidays together. They argued sometimes, particularly about aesthetics when choosing wall colors, about Babak's former partner, and about where to go on trips. Sunil feels connected to Babak, enjoys his company, and thinks he's someone he'd like to spend his life with. But, despite all of these experiences, Sunil has thoughts about whether his relationship with Babak would last: do I really love him? Is he the person I want to marry? Sunil would like to be sure that Babak is a solid partner for him and to be sure about his own feelings.

Of course, it would be nice if we knew in advance exactly how a dish at a restaurant will taste, whether a person is a good partner for us 100 percent of the time, how our manager will behave at work, which city we should move to for school, or when a pet is going to get sick.

But, despite your dynamic mind working really hard to figure things out with clarity, come up with new information to help you make decisions, or help you arrive at the perfect solution, it's impossible to eliminate completely the fact that you just don't know how things will go, what's going to happen in the next minute, or how things will unfold in your life.

How does it feel for you to handle all of life's uncertainty? How does it feel for you to realize that, basically, there is stuff you know, stuff you know you don't know, and tons of stuff that you don't know you don't know?

As a high achiever, it's possible that you feel ambiguity and a push to solve ambiguity, unknowns, and uncertainty a couple of notches higher than a person who is not prone to doing things right and perfect. It's possible that when something is deeply important to you, you would rather know everything, eliminate uncertainty, and minimize doubt as quickly as possible. You might prefer to know the outcome of an ambiguous situation – even if the outcome is negative – rather than face uncertainty.

Here is the tricky part: you may do all types of things to reduce uncertainty – searching for information, reading all books on a topic, watching all documentaries related to a project, and so on – but not every action is going to help you to expand your life and be who you want to be.

As much as we would love to know everything we need to know, that's an impossible task for any human being. The reality is that we make our best guesses based on the information we have in a given moment, anticipating what's possible to anticipate, and acknowledging that we don't have control over what the future holds.

Pause and Play

Here are the micro-skills you can practice to effectively navigate those uncertain moments:

- Notice which situations have made you feel ambivalent, doubtful, and uncertain today.
- Stay with the feelings of uncertainty and ambiguity the best you can: describe them, name them, and say "yes" to them.

  (You can go back to Chapter 32, Terrible Feelings, and Chapter 33, Pleased to Meet You!, as a reference)

- Use acceptance mini-prompts when facing uncertain feelings.

  You can tell yourself things like: "I want to try my hardest at this moment to ride this wave of uncertainty; I want to do what I can to let this fear of not knowing come and go."

- You can listen to podcast episode 25 on uncertainty on the website www.playingitsafe.zone.

43 Undoing Decidophobia

Choice 1: searching through more than 100 dating profiles
Choice 2: looking at the menu at an Italian restaurant
Choice 3: scanning through countless types of nails to hang a painting at home
Choice 4: researching hundreds of types of mattresses
Choice 5: choosing the best title for a chapter of your manuscript
Choice 6: exploring the destination for your next vacation
Choice 7: deciding who to invite to your birthday party
Choice 8: choosing a name for your baby
Choice 100: . . .
Choice 1,000: . . .
Choice 10,000: . . .
Choice nnnnnnnnn: . . .

How often do you have to make choices, decisions, and resolutions in your day?

Quite likely, it's very often – too often – every day because that's the time we're living in. And how do you handle those deciding moments?

- Do you spend hours playing out in your mind the best choices, smartest decisions, and most efficient ways to complete a task?
- Do you struggle to decide because you might make a bad decision and regret it later?
- Do you play out in your head all kinds of what-if scenarios about things that could possibly go wrong to help you make the best decision?
- Do you check all the best resources before making a choice?
- Are you afraid that a better option might come your way after you've made up your mind about something?
- Do you second- or third-guess yourself when having to make a choice?

If you answered yes to three or more of these questions, you may be dealing with decision-phobia – also referred as decidophobia, decision paralysis, or indecision paralysis. The bottom line is that it's hard for you to make choices, from the simple ones, like what type of tea to buy, to the complex ones, like whom you should marry.

Barry Schwartz (2004), an organizational psychologist, has described two types of decision makers: maximizers and satisficers. Maximizers strive to make the best decision possible, so they collect and optimize all the information needed with that purpose in my mind. Satisficers consider their gains and losses in a given situation, evaluate their options, and make a decision.

Which one describes you? Do you like to gather as much information as possible about your options so you can make the optimal decision? Or do you make a decision when you find a suitable "good-enough" option and move on?

In general, it's annoying to make a bad decision – but it is much more bothersome when you are genuinely invested in that choice and what it means to you. In fact, when people care deeply about things and strive to do things perfectly, they get very fearful of making wrong, poor, and thoughtless choices, so, as a result, they spend countless hours analyzing, mulling over, and scrutinizing every potential path they could take.

Do you know what I mean?

Think about it: when you care deeply about something, don't you want to make the best decision possible? Don't you want to exhaust all the possibilities and make sure you have all the information needed to make an optimal decision? And then, do you go on and on, searching, researching, and acquiring as much information as possible to the point that it's overwhelming?

What are the decisions you had to make in the last six months that caused you distress, sleeping difficulties, and hours of time spent in your head?

What are the things your dynamic mind tells you that cause you to dwell on decisions?

It all makes sense. Our human minds do human things. And our dynamic minds are vulnerable to the all types of thinking traps: if I don't carefully think this through, then bad things will happen, and I'll regret it later. So, your mind will often come up with reasons to think and think and think again, all the way through. And yet, where does it lead you?

Think about the times you've gone to a store and, after hours of investigating and examining, left without buying anything.

It's been reinforced with our dynamic minds that they should hold onto a system that makes sense (e.g., thinking and thinking about a situation) – and yet, check in with yourself about how it impacts the relationships you have with yourself, with others, and with the things you care about. You may have tried things like listing pros and cons when making a decision, but when something matters to you, it's quite unlikely that a pros-and-cons analysis is going to be helpful. You need to get to the root of your difficulty with making decisions.

Here are some reasons decision-making might be hard for you: (1) you're afraid of making the wrong decision and screwing things up;

(2) you're afraid of missing a better choice later on; (3) you are hooked on thoughts about making the right, perfect, and flawless choice; (4) you're afraid of the feelings of regret, sorrow, and remorse that may come with a given choice; (5) you're holding onto thoughts about a decision that may reflect who you are or what you're worth.

> **Pause and Play**
>
> Instead of spinning out in your head and listening to all the intellectualizing thoughts your dynamic mind will come up with in these situations, play the workability game!
>
> When you find yourself overthinking, dwelling on, and mulling over a decision (no matter how big or small) that you need to make, try the following micro-skills:
>
> - Ask yourself: what's my dynamic mind guarding me from if I don't make the best choice?
> - Go back to your precious values: what really matters when making this choice?
> - Notice and name those intellectualizing thoughts for what they are (e.g., Mr. Thinker, Ms. Reasoning, and so on).
> - Watch out for your decision style: maximizer or satisficer.
> - Set a time limit for searching for information.
> - Set a deadline for any decision you have to make.
> - Set which variables or factors will help determine your choice (instead of dealing with countless criteria).
> - Approach each decision as a process (not a life-and-death situation).
>
> And keep in mind that despite what most people might think about maximizers making better decisions, Schwartz's research demonstrated that creating many choices impedes our ability to make decisions, triggers excessive searching, and, in fact, leads us to make worse choices (Schwartz, 2004; Yang & Chiou, 2010).

44 Tackling Procrastination

When Robin works on his personal website, he usually sits down at his computer, starts working on the fonts, colors, and layout, and then, after a couple of minutes, starts having thoughts like: it's not worth showing my work; it's not ready yet. What if people don't give me jobs because of it? What if people get the wrong impression of my work because of the layout? This isn't the right yellow; I need to check other shades and get the right one so it really conveys what my work is about. After two to three hours of going back and forth with himself, he has a headache and doesn't publish his website.

Two hours later, when his agent calls, he quickly says, "Let's move the date to the end of the month; I'll do my best to have it done by then."

There is this idea that having high standards will help you get things done well. While there is some truth to that, it's also true that fear, worry, and anxiety are drivers for postponing decisions, projects, or commitments. Your mind might come up with all types of thoughts about what you can and cannot do. Sometimes – not all the time – procrastination and perfectionism go hand in hand, especially when you're doing something you care about.

Many times, we either get so engaged in our own minds that we miss the consequences of not taking action or we get so engaged in the possibility of things going badly that we're paralyzed by distress. Let's break this down:

When Robin sits at his desk to work on his website, it's very easy for him to imagine how it could look, the impact it could have on his career, and how good it will feel to see the website with the qualities he envisions for it. It feels so good to think about those imagined attributes of the website that Robin doesn't engage at all with the costs of not getting the website done – so he continues pursuing a perfect look for it rather than getting it done.

This particular thinking process is called *omission bias*. Think about it: it feels so good for Robin to continue visualizing his website that he lets that particular feeling reinforce his repetition of the same actions – paying attention to the nitty-gritty details and chasing that perfect unique look – while omitting considering the impact of not completing the task, not taking action, and not getting it done.

Other times, Robin sits at his desk and imagines what could happen if he doesn't successfully complete his website with the particular look he's searching for – how many contracts he'd lose, how his students wouldn't respect him and may see him as a fraud, how he might be unable to provide for his family, and how his career would be a failure. In these moments, Robin gets hooked on anticipating the worst-case scenario and doesn't get any work done on his website.

Robin genuinely wants to have a website that properly reflects his artistic style, creative work, and personality. Yet he either gets lost in searching for the perfect look for it or imagining the disaster of not getting it right. Either way, it causes him to keep postponing the website's publication date, and he ends up feeling stressed, embarrassed when his friends ask him about it, and critical of himself for not getting it done.

So procrastination is a word that, when you're doing something important to you, it might be masking two thinking traps: omission bias or anticipating a worst-case scenario (also known as omission fallacy or anticipating catastrophic disasters, respectively).

It makes sense that you'd want to make sure nothing goes wrong. But what happens when you buy into the thoughts, "I'll do this tomorrow; I'll take care of this later; I don't need to do this now"? Does it help to get you where you want to go?

Pause and Play

Moving forward, so you can keep doing what works, you need to go where your mind tells you that you cannot go. You can even anticipate what your dynamic mind is going to say and name those thoughts. For example: here comes my fortune-telling mind.

Instead of postponing and postponing, or planning how you're going to postpone something, try the following tips – not necessarily in this order:

- Visualize the steps you need to take for a particular task (don't visualize the end goal, only the steps).
- Use the STING method to get things done: Select one task at a time, Time yourself, Ignore everything else, take No breaks in that window of time, and Give yourself a reward (King, 2018).
- If needed, combine fun steps with tedious ones, one after another.
- Find an encouraging, caring, and supportive person that you can check in with on a regular basis about your progress.

- Investigate what's truly important to you by asking yourself the question: will doing this enrich my life? (If not, then procrastinating on it doesn't really matter.) But if so, then clarify for yourself: what about this is important to me? If I do it, how will it improve my life? What values will I be living?
- Instead of pushing away the fear of making mistakes, make room for it; don't get tired of describing how it feels in your body and naming it.

45 Tough Love!

Peter, a self-taught baker and pastry chef, decided to spend the afternoon making a delicious chocolate and coffee tartlet. This recipe includes chocolate and coffee custard, a soft tart crust, and whipped cream and chocolate shavings on top. The tartlet is one of his favorite recipes because, to him, it's the perfect combination of sweet and crispy together.

As he usually does, Peter tasted the custard to make sure it had the right flavor and texture; he couldn't help but notice that it wasn't there yet. He knows exactly how it needs to taste so it will melt in your mouth when everything is combined. He kept mixing, adding a bit more sugar, and trying it again. But every time the mix reached his mouth, he was still dissatisfied with its flavor.

Peter's internal monologue started sounding like this: *try again! You can do better than this! Do Better. You cannot serve it like this. You're being lazy! You cannot give up. You cannot settle for this flavor! Are you an idiot? It looks like this is your first time making this recipe!*

Peter ended up throwing out the custard and preparing a new one; he wasn't sure what messed up the flavor the first time, but he couldn't use that batch for his precious chocolate and coffee tartlet. He carefully measured the same ingredients, added them to the bowl, and mixed them – and when he tried the new batch, the enjoyment on his face showed that this new filling was a success. With great enthusiasm, Peter filled the tartlet with this custard, added whipped cream and chocolate shavings on the top, and finished the dessert with a delicate mint leaf on the side.

One could easily say that Peter's internal dialogue was motivational and helpful because, when he was done, he had prepared a new mix, felt much better about the quality of it, and was assured by the results of his work.

Sure, sometimes tough love gets us moving and doing things. But what happens when our mind sounds like our worst enemy and we get hooked on these pushy thoughts, bullying comments, and harsh commands?

Imagine for a moment that you're next to Peter and you hear all those tough thoughts cycling through his mind – what would you tell him?

There is a slippery slope between being tough on yourself and opening the door to hours of self-criticism, rumination, feeling down, and

DOI: 10.4324/9781003083153-52

ashamed of yourself. There is also a difference between holding yourself accountable for what you do and treating yourself as if you don't matter.

Have all the times you were tough on yourself gotten you moving and doing the things that are important to you? What happened to your relationship with yourself during these times?

It's already hard to feel stuck, to make mistakes, and to not get things the way we want them; but adding a layer of harsh criticisms is like adding salt to an open wound.

Chronic self-criticism can easily lead you to feel more discouraged, more anxious, more ashamed; even if you don't fully believe any of those self-criticisms, the way you talk to yourself impacts how you feel about yourself in those moments. The more you criticize yourself, the more emotionally drained you will feel.

Letting go of trying to motivate yourself with bullying thoughts doesn't mean that you won't try hard, you won't give your best, or you'll stop caring about your performance. It just means that you will choose to relate to yourself in those moments in a much more helpful way so that, in the long run, you can do more and more of the things that are deeply important to you.

Pause and Play

When your dynamic mind attempts to motivate you with tough love, see if instead of pushing yourself to do more, better, and faster, or getting hooked on those harsh thoughts, you can:

- Make a 24-hour commitment to practice patience with yourself.
- Ask for help, if needed.
- Remind yourself that, in those moments, you're doing the best you can.

    (Please notice the words "in those moments," because the reality is that our best efforts vary from situation to situation; they're never permanent.)

- Label those tough thoughts as "thinking, thinking, thinking."
- Go back to Chapter 32, Terrible Feelings, and Chapter 33, Pleased to Meet You!, for tips for handling uncomfortable emotions.

46 Let's Move

Questions for you:

- If a person that knows you very well were standing next to you and described how you relate to your body, health, and physical fitness, what would they say?
- On a scale from 1 to 10, 1 being the least and 10 the most, how would you rank yourself in regard to how you value your health? Are you close to 10? Somewhere close to it? Are you far from it? How far?
- Are you taking care of yourself the way you really want to?

If you're close to 10, kudos to you. If you're far from it or not where you want to be, then it's time to step back and do something about it. You're reading this book because you want to change something; this is a chance to do so. It may not be the perfect time, and your dynamic mind may be coming up with hundreds of reasons why you cannot do it – and yet, there won't ever be an ideal time. Just start exactly where you are.

Before you get cranky with me and close the book, hear me out: this chapter won't be a collection of clichés about lifestyle, diet, or workout routines. It's pretty well established that our physical and mental health matter, and it's also pretty well established that despite all the effort we put into it, health-related changes are difficult to make.

So, instead of preaching or listing all the ways you can improve your health, I'm asking you to consider two things:

(1) Your values. There are many variables fueling our physical health challenges, and this issue often carries a lot of weight from our personal histories. That's why the most well-thought-out recipes for lifestyle change can fall flat. Figuring out your health-related values, what matters to you, and why those things are important are actually much more consequential parts of building a fulfilling life. The "hows" will come, but being clear about the drivers behind your choices will help you make more workable, long-lasting, and valuable decisions.

Check in with yourself for a moment: what would you like your best friend to say about how you relate to your health? Instead of rushing through your answer, give yourself a moment to pause and then answer the question.

Ben, a cosmetic dentist, asked himself that question when his doctor told him he was prediabetic. He didn't like the idea of changing his diet, dropping sweets, or reducing the number of glasses of wine he drinks at the end of the day. But, when he asked himself the question, what would you like your best friend to say about how you relate to your health?, Ben noticed a soft thought in his mind about how he wants to celebrate his grandchildren's birthdays, how he wouldn't want his relatives to see that life was happening to him, and how special it would be to be fully present with them. Ben discovered that more than blindly going along with the recommendations from the doctor, he was choosing to be physically present with himself so he could be present for the ones he loves.

(2) Physical activity. We have been told that being physically active gives us an endorphin rush, influences our brain chemicals, and helps protect our bodies from illness. So far, so good. But what if being physically active does much more than that? What if all these health messages are too minimal and don't unpack the other important layers that come with physical activity?

When I was a teenager, my native country, Bolivia, experienced the departure of a military regime and the emergence of a democratic government. My friends and classmates and I were singing and dancing to songs by Charly García, Enanitos Verdes, and others, songs about dreams, hope, oppression, love, and freedom; these were sweet times we had together. When I was navigating hormonal challenges in my early twenties and surviving those annoying mood shifts that happen out of the blue when your hormone levels are a bit all over the map, dancing to music of the 80s and 90s – Depeche Mode, U2, Radiohead – gave me opportunities to reset my mind.

When facing the sadness, frustration, and grief that comes with breakups and ruptures in relationships, moving my body to the songs of romantic singers like Chayanne or Ricky Martin made the situations feel more manageable.

When dealing with the pressures of grad school, dancing salsa, rumba, and reggaeton for a couple of hours on a Friday evening gave me the strength I needed to continue pursuing my education.

When adjusting to the responsibilities of finishing my postdoctoral training and applying for jobs, practicing yoga every Sunday morning and listening to soft classical music in the background gave my body the opportunity to stretch itself and relax.

The unspoken, or ignored, benefits of moving our bodies – dancing, running, swimming, cycling – are connecting with others, regulating our moods, gathering inspiration, stimulating our brains, supporting each other, creating community rituals, and continuing what our ancestors have been doing since time immemorial: moving their bodies collectively and surviving with the support of others.

We are born to move.

> **Pause and Play**
>
> As you keep playing the workability game and creating the life you want to live, here are three questions for you to consider:
>
> 1. What are your values going to be regarding your health?
> 2. What's the song you're going to move your body to today?
> 3. How are you going to listen to what works for your body?

47 To Quit or Not to Quit

Never, ever, ever give up!!!!
Winners never quit.
When the going gets tough, the tough get going.
Doing what matters comes with sacrifices.

I wonder how many books and social-media posts end with sentiments like these, how many necklaces and bracelets have words like these carved on them, or how often caring friends tell us something similar. Probably thousands.

My grandmother grew up in a family of nine children and became an orphan at age 18; she was the only female and the oldest child. When her parents passed away, one after the other, they asked her to make sure that each one of her brothers finished high school and obtained a college degree. She promised them that she would. So, starting at age 18, my Mama Panza, as I called her, was in charge of her brothers; she went to college to become a teacher and managed a full house.

Many years later, I listened to the stories of how persistent and strict she was, and how diligent with all the different tasks she managed; she never forgot the promise she made to her parents. Among the many nuggets of advice she shared with all her grandchildren, one that stuck in my mind was, "When you fall down, you stand up and you keep walking."

Yes, perseverance, grit, and determination have undoubtedly been critical to so many discoveries, creations, and truly extraordinary achievements and developments in all areas of knowledge.

When a goal matters to us, we don't hesitate to put in the extra hours needed to reach it; we push ourselves to achieve quality work and surround ourselves with people who get things done with the same level of commitment.

How many times have you pushed yourself relentlessly when you were passionate about something?

Angela Duckworth (2016), a social psychologist, has studied the difference between people who succeed and those who don't. Her research shows that talent, skill, and ability are not guarantors of success; they're helpers, but there isn't a cause-and-effect relationship between your ability to do something and your success in completing it. Duckworth has strongly suggested that grit, or focused persistence, is the key variable differentiating these two groups of people.

The truth is that passionate people, high achievers, and individuals that care deeply about something are more vulnerable to an excessive attachment to grit. Think about it: how often does your mind engage with thoughts about reaching your potential, pursuing your passions, following your long-term goals, or always challenging yourself.

If I were hanging out with my grandmother in the kitchen, watching as she stirred a stew and added cilantro to it, and I shared with her the thoughts I mentioned earlier, I'm almost sure she would reply: there is value in doing something important, and doing it well, even when it's hard.

Perseverance is necessary for all of us to thrive in life. But what happens when we keep pushing ourselves without checking in to see how things are working in our relationships with others and ourselves? Does it work for you to keep going and going without stepping back and assessing whether you're pursuing something that is burning you out or revitalizing you?

Our values and the things that matter to us can also take us into a pit of despair, a waterfall of frustration, or a cage of anger. This might sound a bit paradoxical and conflicting; you may be wondering how our values can make us suffer if they're what give our lives meaning. Grab your favorite drink and hear me out.

As I've said before, humans do human things. And one human thing to do is to find what gives our lives meaning, purpose, and passion, and to hold onto those things with white knuckles. It's not our fault. It's in our makeup to not just survive but also to flourish, thrive, and grow. So, when we experience meaning, we want more of it, and we relentlessly keep doing whatever it is that keeps us on that path.

But when we're in this mode, which game are we playing? Are we playing the workability game or are we playing the game of perfectly living our values?

Living an unchecked life, even when doing what matters to us, is like walking into a minefield – we don't know when things are going to explode.

Have you watched the movie *Finding Nemo*? If you haven't, please mark this page and go watch it before you continue reading. I mean it. This tiny movie-break will help you make sense of this chapter.

If you have watched the movie...

You know that in this Pixar film, Nemo loses his mother abruptly and, as a result, his father, Marlin, strengthens his parenting duties and grows overprotective. As Nemo gets older and starts attending school, he wants to explore more in the ocean and hang out with his friends, but Marlin is worried about his safety. As the story keeps moving, you see all the adventures that Nemo and Marlin experience separately – shark attacks, coral, blue whales, swimming in the East Australian current, a fish tank in a dentist's office – and it's undoubtedly clear that Marlin is committed to protecting, loving, and caring for Nemo at all costs, all the time, all the way.

But Marlin is so attached to his parenting value of protecting Nemo that he doesn't look at how his actions are impacting Nemo, their relationship, and his own ability to parent effectively.

Our passions are like vitamins that nourish our quests for meaningful lives, but – here's a really big "but" – if they go unchecked, they can be a source of pain, struggle, and misery in the long run.

Seth Godin (2007), an entrepreneur, has introduced the notion of "the dip" as the representation of those moments in between peaks of excitement and long-term success of a project. You may have had many of those moments that make you want to quit, like the fifth time you go for an interview and don't get a callback, the eighth time you perform with your band in the middle of nowhere, the tenth time you attempt to cook a meal and end up with a flavorless dish, or the twentieth gathering you try to have with your in-laws where they don't get back to you for months.

And as Godin pinpointed, "extraordinary benefits accrue to the tiny minority of people who are able to push just a tiny bit longer than most. Extraordinary benefits also accrue to the tiny majority with the guts to quit early and refocus their efforts on something new."

Going back for a moment to my grandmother: she often shared stories with us over dinner about how she had to choose every single day whether to spend time with her four kids as they grew older or prepare the next day's agenda for the groups of teachers she worked with. She described feeling pulled between one and the other and at times not knowing the right thing to do. She was afraid of not spending quality time with her kids and she was afraid of not being prepared for work.

Have you had moments like the ones my grandma described? How did it feel for you to experience that values conflict?

Living and doing what matters to us is never a clean, perfect, or easy path. It's rocky and hard, and it invites you to check over and over whether it's the right time to quit or the wrong time. But quitting something you're invested in is never easy. It's difficult to end a relationship, to let go of a writing project, to resign from a project that you started, or to choose not to work overtime to get things done the way you would like.

I'm not saying that you should quit, abandon something, or discontinue working when things get hard, rocky, or challenging. I'm saying that if something is sucking the life out of you, you may need to check in with yourself to see what you need to let go or do less of – or even do more of. I'm saying that pushing through hard times and quitting are two sides of living your values.

Here are some things that coud make it hard for you to quit: (1) you're hooked on the thought "I shouldn't quit" or a variation of it; (2) you're avoiding an uncomfortable emotion; (3) you're attached to a single goal as the only way to live a value; (4) you're not stepping back and checking how a particular pursuit is impacting you. Or, as my friend Rob Archer, an organizational psychologist, noted: (5) you have an unclear situation, with strong pros and cons and values-consistent reasons on both sides.

> ### Pause and Play
>
> To keep cultivating your drive for high achievement without losing yourself I encourage you to:
>
> - Step back often and check if you're living your values flexibly or rigidly.
> - Check in with yourself to see if living a particular value is sucking the life out of you.
> - Ask yourself what quitting means to you.
> - Check in with yourself: who are you without the doing? If you stop pursuing a goal, what's there for you to feel and sit with?
> - What are other ways for you to live that value if you let go of a particular goal or activity?
>
> When making these decisions, some things will stay, some things will have to go, and some things will need to take up less space in your schedule – but in each one of these choices, you're opening the door for incredible things to come your way. You may feel like collapsing when you cut something from your life – it's painful to do – so I want to close this chapter with an edited version of my Mama Panza's saying:
>
> When you fall down, stand up and keep walking with gentleness, compassion, and kindness toward yourself, in every step you take.

48 Finding Your Rhythm

When you care about something, of course you want to give it your best – and you give your best by putting your head, heart, and hands to work. Giving your best also means putting your time, energy, and mental resources into it. And it also means going into go-go-go mode many times, one project after another and one task after another.

It's a precious thing to care deeply about the things we do, for sure. What would life be without our passions, wants, and aspirations? They're strong forces we use to navigate through many moments in our lives; they keep us moving, give us meaning, and point us toward our values.

But what happens when we keep moving without pausing to check how we're living? What happens when we keep going and going, driven by our passions, without checking our rhythm, pace, and speed? What happens when we go and go without reflecting, learning, and adjusting? What happens when we keep withdrawing from the bank account of life without making any deposits on it?

If your mind is thinking, "Oh boy, here she comes with the speech about finding balance, the classic life-work balance," I'm sorry to disappoint your mind, but I'm definitely not going in that direction. Instead, I'm headed toward what behavioral science has to offer us about go-go-go mode, just for a little bit.

Well-known organizational psychologist Adam Grant (Schwantes, 2018; World Economic Forum, 2020) has questioned multiple times the notion of life-work balance. The reality is that no matter how popular this idea has become, it's a myth. Here's why: when we truly care about something, our schedule is not balanced in terms of the number of hours we spend hanging out with friends and family and participating in other things that are important to us.

Think for a moment about your own day-to-day life: how often do you achieve this life-work balance everyone is talking about? How often do you find yourself worrying about overly focusing on one area and abandoning others? How often do you criticize yourself for not having life-work balance, as if something is wrong with you? How often do you feel the stress of striving to get things done under a deadline?

When we buy into the idea of having life-work balance, we dream about getting work done in four hours so we can then relax and devote

DOI: 10.4324/9781003083153-55

four hours to hanging out with our significant other. We picture having a perfect balance, a perfect equipoise, a perfect equilibrium among the things, relationships, responsibilities, and tasks that are part of our lives.

The truth is that there may be times when that symphony of people, time, and activities that constitutes our lives gets harmoniously organized. But most of the time, it's a tuneless, dissonant, and discordant collection of the things we do and the time we expend on them.

Life-work balance is a fantasy goal, period. Instead of striving for it, Grant suggests that it's more important we find our life-work rhythm.

To find your life-work rhythm, I invite you to consider two variables:

(1) How you get things done, naturally!

Steve Pavlina (2012) explains that, when we're getting things done, we employ one of two natural strategies (or we use them in combination with one another): plodding and bursting.

- Plodding means that you continue doing things with a steady and stable workflow, day after day. Here is an example of plodding: Stephen King (Atkins, 2016) writes about 1,000 words every single day, at the same time and in the same place.
- Bursting means that you work in short, temporary cycles of focused, intense, and targeted work. For instance, Sylvester Stallone (Commaandco, 2018) wrote the initial 90-page script of *Rocky* in three days.

So, ask yourself: how do I naturally, spontaneously, and effortlessly work?

(2) How you can be consistent and flexible at the same time!

Have you ever seen runners training for a marathon? Some of them run every day for a specific number of weeks or months. Others run every other day. Others run with a certain frequency – say, two to three days in a row – take a break of the same length, and then pick it up again. Is that wrong? Does the frequency of a runner's practice runs determine their chances of winning a race?

What are the tips, messages, and recommendations you have heard about consistency? Quite likely, most of them are some version of, "You need to show up all the time. Consistency is the key to success. Showing up is half the battle."

But what really happens when you push yourself to show up unfailingly, always, and reliably to what you said you were going to do, without considering other life circumstances? What happens if you push yourself to work regularly while one of your best friends is going through a breakup, your pet is sick, or your partner is struggling with the kids?

Life is always happening, and rarely do we have the chance to choose what comes our way. Unexpected, unplanned, and unforeseen situations happen out of the blue. And when those moments occur, they invite us to revisit again this idea of "100 percent consistency."

Instead of holding tightly onto thoughts of "always showing up," and variations on these thoughts, you may want to consider approaching things with flexible consistency (sounds like an oxymoron, right?).

Flexible consistency is about creating a consistent schedule to get things done in a way that is adjustable, adaptable, and changeable; basically, it's about creating a schedule that is context-based and not rule-based.

For instance, Fred was a podcaster who spent years developing his show; he was very careful about the quality of his audio, the platforms he used, the people he interviewed, and which themes he focused on. He had released three episodes a week for the last eight years. After releasing each episode, he would check all his social media channels so he could reply to comments. He prepared the coming week's content every Saturday morning. As his audience grew, he approached some sponsors and strived to send them a quarterly report on the performance of the show. Every year, Fred took online classes on creativity, audio innovations, storytelling, and other relevant topics so that he would always be up-to-date and could deliver the best content possible and with the best quality.

One Saturday morning, as he was making notes on his yellow notepad, he answered a call from his wife; he knew something was wrong when he could only hear his wife's rapid breathing. He kept asking what was wrong, and she finally said, "Fred, our son has had a car accident and we need to identify his body." Fred felt in that instant as if his whole world collapsed; a buzzing in his ears blocked any other sounds, his body felt light, and he felt as if he were dreaming.

For the next two weeks, Fred went through the motions of preparing his son's funeral, eating a little bit, consoling his wife, and reliving memories of time spent with his 15-year-old. During that time, he continued releasing three podcast episodes a week and continued replying to comments. Fred was hooked on the thought that "consistency is key, always."

Acknowledging your preferred style – plodding or bursting – for getting things done, or figuring out what style better fits a project, and organizing your schedule based on what's happening in your life will help you find a long-lasting rhythm for doing the things that matter to you.

Pause and Play

There is no one way or the perfect way of making things happen and doing what matters; there are so many ways to do so. If you're a maker, a doer, a creator, a person with a good track record, or a person that makes things happen, you know how it feels to be preoccupied with getting things done. The key is to do these things without burning yourself out.

Here are some questions to ponder:

- How can you organize your values-based life into a well-orchestrated rhythm, from the time you wake up to the time you go to sleep?
- Which values-based projects can be done in bursting mode?
- Which values-based moves can be done in plodder mode?
- How can you move from push-and-pull mode, where you strive to do more work, faster, and with excellent quality, to doing what you care about, at a high level, without burning yourself out?
- How can you create a seasonal schedule for doing what you care about?

49 Little Tidbits

Have you watched the movie *Inception*? If you're interested in science fiction, I highly recommend it. The film is directed by Christopher Nolan; you may know him from his other movies, which include *Batman Begins*, *The Prestige*, and *The Dark Knight*. Without spoiling the movie for you, I'm just going to say that *Inception* explores the idea of unpacking our unconscious minds through our dreams and mixes reality and dreams, reality within dreams, and dreams without reality throughout the whole story.

It has been said that it took Nolan ten years to write the script for *Inception*, polish it, and give it the desired flow. If you have watched the movie, you can see how much effort it must have taken to create, design, and construct all the visual worlds; the degree of detail in each one is just astonishing. Can you imagine what the visual board must have looked like to manage and keep track of all the movie's elements? Can you imagine the list of visual effects, shots, audio effects, set elements, and edits – and the countless other things that must have been involved in the filming process? How would you feel arriving to work on this film every day for two years?

The reality is that the more you care about something, the more you will experience the push and pull of wanting to do it perfectly, to push harder and harder, to check and re-check, and to do more and more. And you will see that – because you care and because it matters to you – the list of things you need to do, take care of, and complete grows and grows.

Think about the different projects you've participated in. How did it feel when you were looking at the tasks involved and all that you needed to do? How often did you feel stressed about not having enough time to complete all the necessary steps? How many times did you have trouble sleeping because your mind kept going over all the things coming your way the following day? How often did you create a to-do list only to realize at the end of the day that you'd only accomplished 10 to 15 percent of the tasks? How often did you get one thing done, drop 15, and neglect ten other important areas of your life?

Let's examine it this way: what does this week look like for you? What are the errands you need to run? How many emails do you need to write and reply to? What decisions do you need to make? What are the things

DOI: 10.4324/9781003083153-56

you need to buy? What activities do you need to plan? What are you doing for your meals?

If you added up the number of hours it would take for you to complete all the tasks, errands, and things you need to do each week, what would you get? Years ago, I asked one of my clients this question, and after realistically looking at her calendar and calculating the number of hours needed for each task, she realized she would need to work 154 hours that week to accomplish everything.

Are we a lot busier than our ancestors were? Did the cavewomen and cavemen have to do as much as we do nowadays? I don't know, but what I do know is that the day has a limited number of hours.

In the previous chapter, Finding Your Rhythm, you read about two different strategies: plotting and bursting, and, hopefully, you now have a better sense of how you naturally tend to do things or which projects may be better fits than others.

And yet, even though you have to figure out your natural style to get things done, many of the activities you participate in may involve a laundry list of steps. For example, preparing a dinner party for your friends requires that you ask everyone for their availability, figure out which time works best, ask each person about their dietary restrictions, find a recipe that everyone can enjoy, check what drinks you have on hand, get groceries, choose a special dessert to surprise everyone, clean your apartment, make the meal, help your friends feel at home once they arrive, enjoy the meal, and then drink a scotch after all that work.

When looking at all the things you need to do, how do you handle all those tasks? How do you handle the stress of having a long list of things to do? How do you organize your tasks for the day? Maybe you're using an app (e.g. Todoist, Apple Calendar, Trello, Evernote, Google Calendar) or a paper and pencil organizer – or maybe you keep track of them in your mental to-do list.

There are so many ways to organize your time these days: time-management coaches to help you to make the most of each day; systems that have been developed exclusively with organization in mind (e.g., *Getting Things Done, 7 Habits of Highly Effective People, Deep Work,* and *The 4-Hour Workweek*); and, in the not-too-distant future, artificial intelligence may even answer questions about organizing your day.

The challenge with all these approaches is that, in general, they focus on accomplishing goals and checking tasks off a to-do list without looking at your personal history as part of your context. Being a go-getter, a high achiever, a self-starter, a perfectionist, or a doer means that you care deeply, and you may do a looooooooot more than other people to meet your standards in many areas of your life. It means that your days are full, packed, and possibly overbooked. It means that you may move from project to project, from meeting to meeting, and from gathering to gathering in the blink of an eye – not necessarily because you're an extrovert but because the way you take care of the things that are important to you means that there is a lot to do.

Don't get me wrong, getting things done, pursuing our goals, and following our passions is lovely and necessary. In fact, this book is about how to live your values without sacrificing your standards. But as I shared in the previous chapter, I'm not sure if pushing-pushing-pushing or doing more and more and more are the only ways to accomplish these things, or if they're even sustainable.

There is no magic wand to eliminate all the errands, phone calls, projects, emails, or the hundreds of other things you need to do. And as much as it feels good to get them done, it's also a recipe for large amount of stress if you don't pause to check how that pace is working for you (ACT style), adjust often to new challenges, and consider what's driving your actions (e.g., are you doing things to mask a fear of failure? Are you chasing the perfect feeling? Are you hoping to be acknowledged in a particular way by others?).

I know how much you want to take care of things, and I deeply respect that. And yet, if go-go-go mode has been your style, and you often find yourself running out of time, you may want to consider other ways of handling projects that feel overwhelming so you can avoid sinking with the feeling that everything is a problem to be solved, immediately, right away, and with urgency.

You can do little tidbits.

Pause and Play

To raise the level of your workability game, you can develop the following micro-skills for dealing with tasks, activities, or situations that feel giant, that cause you to lose sleep, or that you have been avoiding:

- Do little tidbits constantly.

    You don't have to do everything at once; see if you can break down a project into small steps. You can break it down any way you want – even a two-minute nibble counts.

- Do little tidbits as a habit.

    Making a habit of doing little tidbits is very helpful. You can support this habit by having a designated place where you complete a task or by creating a routine. And you can also make it difficult to get out of doing a task (e.g., if you avoid tasks by getting on email, close your email, and turn off the notifications. If you get distracted by the TV, what about hiding it?).

- Make your progress visible.

    When approaching tasks we care about but have been avoiding, it helps to find ways to track what we've done so far and make it visible. Teresa Amabile, a researcher at Harvard Business School, found that tracking the progress of important tasks keeps us stay more engaged with them. Now, just to be clear, this tracking system doesn't have to be fancy; as long as it's visible and easily accessible, it's great.

If you feel overwhelmed, instead of powering through your tasks and rushing through things, try navigating your day with help from these tidbits:

(a) Choose a values-based activity for the day.

> Focus on one area of your life for the day – relationships, career, personal growth, spirituality, health – and choose a specific activity to do.

(b) Choose one must-do activity.

> Among all the things you need to do, choose one single to-do item that must get done.

(c) Choose one self-care activity that is soothing.

> Busy days also require fun, enjoyment, and pleasure to reset your brain, recharge your batteries, and replenish your energy. Ask yourself, what's one thing you can do to relax – and then do it.
>
> Rich lives have multiple sources of experiences, and a rested mind can do much better work than a fatigued one.

50 Sweet Contradictions

Jess walked into his apartment holding a carrier bag; he was excited to have his newly adopted kitty, Sidney, with him. He'd waited months for Sidney to be ready for adoption, and, finally, he could bring him home. Upon entering the apartment, Jess felt the joy of Sidney checking out his new environment – but he was also afraid that Sidney might not get along with his old dog, Pit.

Nahir was thrilled to meet her in-laws for the first time and was also terrified they might not like her.

Gordon was excited about playing basketball professionally but also felt resentful about all the time it took him away from family trips, vacations, and gatherings.

Gordon, Nahir, and Jess were feeling contradictory, opposite, or different emotions about their individual situations. We often expect that we should have clear, well-defined, and precise feelings about everything, but, unfortunately, that's just not how it usually works. In the chapters Fleeting Feelings, Terrible Feelings, and Pleased to Meet You!, you read about the richness of our emotional experiences.

We're born to feel and to experience all types of emotions, but when being a high achiever, you may believe that you should be clear about what you feel, so that you can make a perfect decision. This implies that there is a right feeling for you to have in every situation.

This fantasy – that there is a right way to feel about things – is called *emotional perfectionism*. Our dynamic minds don't help with this either because, by nature, every thought our minds come up with is an attempt to define, classify, or categorize our internal experiences as either "this" or "that." And on top of it all, if you have a low tolerance for uncertainty and strong need for closure, then you may experience a stronger urge to have emotional clarity at all times.

Igor was just promoted at work, he bought a new home for his parents, and he's awaiting the arrival of his second child. He knows that his life is moving in the direction of what's important to him, so when he gets to feeling a bit down, he immediately chides himself: *What's wrong with me? Why am I feeling this way? I should be grateful for and happy about what I have.* Then he feels guilty for being ungrateful.

DOI: 10.4324/9781003083153-57

Think about your day-to-day life: how often do you feel contradictory things about a dessert? How often do you feel emotionally confused about a relationship? How often do you feel conflicted about your next move at work? How often do you feel ambivalent about a political candidate?

It's human to have contradictory emotional experiences co-existent, side-by-side.

Quite likely, no matter how old you are, where you live, or what you do for a living, you have found yourself in moments of conflict between the demands from conflicting emotions, or the confusing feelings between addressing your own needs or those of others. But if you get hooked on thoughts about the "right" feelings, and chase those feelings, it makes it much harder for you to navigate uncertainty, ambiguity, and unknowns. It makes it challenging for you to have feelings without being consumed by them. And it makes it hard for you to reach conclusions regarding your values.

> **Pause and Play**
>
> Try honing these micro-skills:
>
> - Be curious about your complex and contradictory emotional experiences without judging them.
>
>   You can ask yourself, *What's this feeling of "x"? What's this feeling of "y"?* and so on.
>
> - Ask yourself, "Am I willing to feel a mixture of conflicted emotions if I'm doing something in the service of my values?"
> - When noticing convoluted emotional experiences, instead of pushing yourself to feel one way or another, try describing the varied emotions by using *and*. For example, you may say, "I'm feeling excited and worried," or "I'm scared and relieved."
> - Do your best to be a witness to all of your thoughts, feelings, and sensations as they are, without trying to force them into particular categories.

51 Sugarcoating Moments

In the Julia Roberts movie *Runaway Bride*, her character, Maggie, is confronted by Richard Gere's character, Ike, for going along with whatever type of eggs her boyfriend at the time liked. So, if Maggie's boyfriend liked soft-boiled eggs, she would immediately like them. If her next boyfriend liked huevos rancheros, that would become her new favorite egg dish. As a result of this confrontation, Maggie spends a full day in the kitchen trying all types of eggs: eggs Benedict, scrambled eggs, sunny-side-up eggs, fried eggs, hard-boiled eggs, poached eggs, and so on.

The history of humanity shows us that we have survived as a species because of our connections with others and through biological adaption. The cavewomen and cavemen learned very early that to overcome their extreme living conditions, they'd need to live as part of a group – and to be part of a group, they'd need to foster relationships with others. What are we without relationships with others?

Over time, we have learned that having richer lives involves having strong connections with others. We don't need to have thousands of friends, but we need to be genuinely accepted, seen, and cared for by others.

But what happens when you do everything you can to be liked, accepted, and loved by others – by going along with their likes and dislikes, apologizing multiple times for mistakes, double-checking to make sure you haven't offended anyone, agreeing with people when you actually disagree, and generally avoiding conflict?

What happens when there is a part of you that carries stories about being unlovable, unworthy, or not-good-enough, and your dynamic mind pushes you to handle these thoughts by doing everything you can to make sure others like you?

What happens when you get hooked onto ruling-thoughts that say that working in a relationship is the same as going along with everything?

What happens when you spend tons of mental resources making sure you don't disappoint anybody?

What happens when you believe that being in a relationship with another person is more important than taking care of the relationship you have with yourself?

DOI: 10.4324/9781003083153-58

Arthur, a musician in his midthirties, has been dating Tim for more than three years. From the beginning of their relationship, Tim has been clear that he wants Arthur to participate in gatherings for his political party and to attend church. Arthur doesn't relate to Tim's political views and is not sure he wants to embrace a religious life; however, he's afraid if he tells Tim these things, Tim will break up with him. So, they go to church every week, celebrate religious holidays, and attend political gatherings together. Arthur feels upset with himself for what he's doing, resents Tim for asking these things of him, doubts his capacity to be in a relationship, and questions his spiritual life. He doesn't know how to talk about these things with Tim, so he avoids fights or disappointing Tim by just going along with his requests. When Tim senses pushback from Arthur about participating in any of the activities, Arthur quickly tells him that it's nothing, that he had a rough day at work or his stomach is upset. Arthur sugarcoats his responses almost mechanically.

The reality is that no one gives us a manual or a blueprint to guide us step-by-step through how to start, cultivate, and grow these relationships; we learn to do so by trial and error. It's not your fault that there is a part of you that deeply wants to feel connected with those around you. It's human, and humans do human things.

As you remember from Chapter 5, All Types of High-Achieving Actions, one of the many areas where perfectionism shows up is relationships – surprise, surprise! Different types of literature have described these behaviors as *people pleasing, fawning, ass-kissing, being a yes-man, being a doormat,* and in other unsympathetic ways. At the end of the day, what's behind these behaviors is that you genuinely care about connecting with others; it's just that obeying all those interpersonal rules without checking how they're working for you in the long term deprives you of experiencing true fulfillment and developing rich relationships with others.

Pause and Play

Playing the workability game will cause you to reflect on how you're living, how you're relating to yourself, and how you're relating to others.

When dealing with sugarcoating behaviors, here are some things you can try:

- Ask yourself, *How are these behaviors working for me in the long term?*
- Check in with yourself to see how those rules about being liked, loved, or accepted by others are working for you.
- Make room for the discomfort that comes from disagreeing with, disappointing, or upsetting others. (You can go back to Chapter 32, Terrible Feelings.)
- Give yourself permission to be honest, real, and genuine with yourself and others. (You can go back to Chapter 40, Tough Choices Need Kindness.)

- When having an urge to act on your sugarcoating behaviors, check in to see what's truly important to you. Go back to your precious values!

If you want a more detailed resource on interpersonal effectiveness, you can check my book *Escaping the Emotional Roller Coaster*. I wrote a couple of chapters on how to assert yourself, be aware of nonverbal communication, identify your attachment style, give and receive feedback, practice empathic behaviors even when you're hurting, and recognize your go-to conflict tactics when dealing with interpersonal discord.

52 O-VER-RE-SPON-SI-BIL-I-TY

When someone is important to us, we go out of our way to make sure that they're okay, we cheer them on, we let them cry on our shoulder when they're struggling, we support them when they want to give up, we understand their needs, and we do what we can to show up for them.

At the heart of our actions lie all the feelings we have for the ones we love. When we care for others, we commit to doing what's best for them; we commit to doing what matters to them; we commit to being next to them.

But when you have a natural tendency to give your best in anything and everyting that's important to you, all the affection you have for others makes you vulnerable to feeling overly responsible for them and their well-being. It's like when you care for others, what happens to them, happens to you; it's as if caring for others makes you responsible for them, accountable to them, and dependable on them. It is as if you respond to their needs as if they were your own.

Daiju, a single, thirty-something photographer, decided to move to a new state for a job. One day, when he was talking to his father on the phone about it, Daiju heard concern in his father's voice about his decision to move; his dad also sounded a bit sad and disappointed. Daiju's father made comments about the importance of family and keeping the family together, and that living in another state makes it difficult to stay connected. Daiju did his best to hear his father's opinions and couldn't stop thinking about what he could say or do to make sure his dad didn't suffer when he moved.

Don, a carpenter, was in a long-term relationship with his high-school sweetheart, Pam. In addition to working as a carpenter, Don also taught on weekends at a trade school. He was the most senior employee at his company, the most accomplished, and the most accountable to his clients. Don was proud of having built his reputation and worked hard to maintain it. He worked when needed, covered shifts for co-workers, and never hesitated to do anything extra to make sure that he always delivered his best to his clients. Don had been waiting for years to become a father, but when Pam got pregnant, a series of health complications and multiple medical appointments required him to be at home most of the time. He felt extremely conflicted because he wanted to show up for

DOI: 10.4324/9781003083153-59

Pam and his child at all times, but he felt guilty because as the "senior" in the company, he felt he should be taking on most of the responsibility for projects – as he had previously been doing.

Miriam had been married to Judith for more than 15 years, had two children, and was a part-time teacher in an elementary school in her neighborhood. Since the beginning of her relationship with Judith, Miriam knew that her parents didn't fully accept Judith – and they never missed an opportunity to point out what they perceived as Judith's faults and voice their disappointment in her being part of the family. Judith knew how Miriam's parents felt about her and often requested that Miriam do something about it. Before every birthday celebration, holiday, family vacation, or casual dinner, Miriam played different scenarios in her mind to try to get her parents and Judith to like one another, connect in some way, or form some sort of relationship. She tried to sit her father next to Judith and start a conversation about soccer (a topic they both enjoyed), she cooked dishes they both liked, and shared different memories that showed she cared for both of them.

Have you had any experiences like Daiju's, Don's, or Miriam's? Do you recall any times when you assumed responsibility for how others felt about you, a situation, or about themselves or each other? Have you felt more responsible for your actions than your peers seem to feel about their own?

It's natural. We all have moments like these because when we care, we do our best to make sure others are okay at all times. But – here comes a big "but" – as much as we hope, want, and wish to have control of others' internal experiences, we don't have control over every single thing we participate in.

When you care about other people and the things you are part of, your mind keeps you busy with all types of thoughts along the lines of, *It's my responsibility to take care of this* or *It's my responsibility to make sure others feel okay*. People who display these over-caring qualities have been described in academic literature as having an *inflated sense of responsibility* or *hyper-responsibility*. It's human, and humans do caring things.

But, for a moment, think about what happens when you put all this pressure on yourself, all the responsibility for others' feelings, and view yourself as the most, and perhaps the only, responsible one in any given situation. What happens if you don't do any of these hyper-responsible actions?

Pause and Play

Playing the workability game offers you opportunities to check what you do, why you do it, and whether or not it works. And that applies to every single thing you do.

When you're struggling with too strong a sense of responsibility, here are things you can do:

- Check what you have control over and what you don't.
- Keep in mind that you don't have control over what people say, do, or feel.
- Ask yourself, *What is my dynamic mind safeguarding me from if I don't engage in these hyper-responsible behaviors?*

It's courageous to care so deeply for others and for the things you do. And yet, checking in with yourself about what's working in every moment will help you to have caring and long-lasting connections with yourself and others.

53   Doing Less, Living More

On a Saturday afternoon, Yusun, a passionate journalist, after cleaning her apartment, taking a quick trip to the grocery store, and watering her Monstera plants, took a quick shower, groomed herself, and sat down for six hours straight in front of her laptop to work with clients in Malaysia. Hour after hour, she asked questions about the intersection of finances, politics, and well-being, listened attentively, and took notes on her iPad, while drinking three bottles of water. The afternoon unfolded, and around 6:23 p.m., she turned off her laptop, fed her puppy, took a deep breath, and turned on the TV to watch one of her favorite movies. Yusun wanted to watch the movie but in the background, her mind was replaying pieces of the interviews from earlier in the day one after another; Yusun tried to focus on different scenes of the movie but couldn't resist pondering about the conversations she had. After two hours of kind of watching the movie, laughing quietly, and drinking a cup of chamomile tea, Yusun called her best friend. They chatted for a bit, and even though Yusun wanted to hear about her best friend's new job, she noticed again how her mind was pulling her into more thinking about her next round of interviews.

Yusun spent the last hour of her day playing with her puppy. While it seemed that she was busy every hour of the day, in the back of her mind she had been organizing her writeup for the interviews, solidifying key points, connecting arguments, deconstructing misconceptions, and slowly having micro-aha moments. Fast forward to the next morning, Sunday: Yusun woke up, brewed coffee, washed her face, and sat down in front of her laptop to write her first article.

Yusun is very committed to journalism. She loves it and doesn't see herself changing careers. In fact, her friends have a running joke about this: they laugh that when they are all one day retired and relaxing on a beach, Yusun will be there... planning her next journal or magazine article.

It's really inspiring to live our passions, to find our purpose, and to do what truly speaks to our heart. I know, for me, once I started living my values, my precious gems, there was no returning to my old ways of being. I have seen the same with my clients: once they get in touch with those life principles they want to live for, and keep moving toward them, everything shifts for them and those around them.

DOI: 10.4324/9781003083153-60

But what happens if you're overly focused on what matters to you at the expense of experiencing, savoring, and appreciating what's happening in front of you? What happens when you're consumed by and overly enthusiastic about something, and ultimately get lost in thinking that the one thing you care about is the only important thing in life?

Doing what matters most requires your full attention, investment, and dedication; that's a fact. Sometimes you may go into full plodding mode to make things happen (see chapter Finding Your Rhythm). And often, you will need to make tough choices.

But doing what matters doesn't necessarily mean that you cannot be present with what's happening around you. It doesn't mean that you cannot be present with the person sitting across from you. It doesn't mean that you cannot be present when watching a movie, relaxing, or having a drink with a friend. In fact, doing what matters in a way that is uplifting, inspiring, and fulfilling requires that you learn the micro-skill of paying flexible attention.

In ACT, we think of paying flexible attention as your ability to be in contact with the present moment with intention (and that's why it's the ACT equivalent of mindfulness). But more than techniques or exercises, paying flexible attention and being in contact with the present moment are attitudes you develop to fully experience life as it's happening; it's like instead of running to "doing land," you stay in "being land."

I could write hundreds of pages citing the benefits of mindfulness and cultivating the skill of being present, but I don't want to bother you with that or turn this chapter into an academic one. I think we can agree that mindfulness has become mainstream, and thousands of books have been written about it; but perhaps most important, it's helpful to keep in mind that we don't need to be monks to cultivate it and we don't need to live in a monastery to practice it.

If you have a formal meditation practice, that's great. But, given the fast pace at which we're living, the endless list of errands on our to-do list, and all the other things we need to do, it's helpful to keep in mind that you can practice to stay in the present moment anytime, anywhere, and with whomever, not just when you're in a quiet space with your eyes closed.

You see, life can get so busy so often that learning to live life is also learning to shift the focus of our attention, intentionally and purposefully, when it matters, when it's useful, and when it's workable.

In Yusun's case, if someone had been next to her, it would have looked like she was watching TV, talking to her friend, and playing with her puppy. But where was her mind? It was trapped in what she had done during the day; clearly, those interviews and her job are important to her – and yet, that conversation with her friend and that play session with her puppy are moments that won't happen again.

Living with purpose invites you to notice when you're distracted, disengaged, or disconnected from what's in front of you. As that song by the Byrds says, "There is a time for everything," and while distraction, daydreaming, and fantasizing can be fun, they're not activities to do all the time.

Check in with your experience: what happens when you're hanging out with friends and, despite being physically there, your mind is running different hypotheses for your next project? Have you ever had an experience where you're watching a movie, and at the end of it you notice that you finished all the cookies that were in front of you? Have you ever tried to read a book while your mind was listing all the reasons to be angry about something that had happened earlier that morning? Have you had moments when your kids were next to you playing and being silly, and half an hour later you realized you couldn't say what they were playing with, what they were saying, and what they were laughing about?

Humans do human things, and being distracted is one of those things we all do. But the more distracted we are, the less life we experience; the more we engage in mindless behaviors, the less satisfying our lives will be; and the more disengaged we are, the less joy we feel.

One of my dear friends, Dr. Russ Harris, author of the book *The Happiness Trap*, likes to talk about savoring our experiences as they occur. Think about how many things happen around us every single moment: the sound of cars, the smell of a cup of tea, the sound of a dog barking, the warmth coming from the electrical heater, the ticktock sound of the clock, the feeling of your partner kissing you goodbye, the sound of the keyboard when typing, or the sensation of the sun on your face when you leave your home. What about starting to notice these things as they happen?

> **Pause and Play**
>
> Doing what works is an invitation to check often where your dynamic mind takes you, what's important in those moments, and when it's helpful or not to be absorbed in our minds.
> Here are some tips for you:
>
> - Open your eyes, ears, and all of your senses to what's happening in front of you.
> - When your mind wanders off into all those thoughts about what you need to do, want to do, and have to do, check where you are and ask yourself if going along with your mind right then is a move toward your values or away from them.
> - When you're doing something that matters to you, it's understandable that your dynamic mind will try to keep you hooked on it 24/7. And yet, your mind is not your boss; it doesn't get to decide where you put your attention and when. That's your choice. And that means that, frequently, you will need to bring

your attention back to what's important to you in that particular moment.
- Build into your day a five-minute window to practice awareness of your experience: set a timer, and, in those five minutes, pay attention to each of your five senses. Describe to yourself – without adding any judgment – what you smell, see, hear, taste, and feel.

You cannot mess up practicing staying in the present because there is no right or wrong way to do it, even though your mind may come up with doubts about what you're doing. As long as you practice noticing and describing what's happening in the moment, intentionally, and bring yourself back to it when your mind wanders, then you're cultivating awareness.

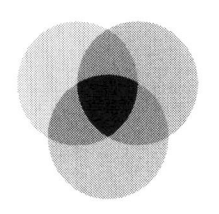

Final Words

Here we are, at the end of the book!

There is one last thing I'm going to share with you, and I promise that I'm not a public relations representative for Malcolm Gladwell. But, if you have been following my work, you know that at some point, I'm going to refer to him.

Malcolm Gladwell has stated many times that our advantages can be our disadvantages and our disadvantages can be our advantages. To me, this sentence captures the beauty, magic, and impact of behavioral science in our day-to-day lives; behavioral science doesn't get caught up in absolutes, in the old way of seeing things as being either black or white, or in the dichotomy of things being either good or bad.

Is it good to pursue high-achieving actions and perfectionistic behaviors because you care deeply about something? The answer, my friend, is: it depends.

As I promised at the beginning of this book, I never asked you to stop doing things that you care deeply about, I never asked you to lower your standards, and I didn't use the classic clichés you may have heard hundreds of times about perfectionism and high-achieving actions. But I did ask you in every chapter to check in with yourself to determine what game you want to play.

I did my best to share with you different micro-skills to maximize, capitalize on, and even augment all those efforts to do the things you care about while enriching, expanding, and living a fulfilling life. I did my best to show you how you can still achieve and excel in what you do without compromising your life.

From the bottom of my heart, I want to encourage you to put into action all the micro-skills you read about in this book, and most important, to keep playing the workability game!

Dr. Z.

PS. An invitation and a reminder for you:

(1) Invitation: If you want to receive weekly tips to get unstuck from procrastination, perfectionism, worries, fears, and anxiety, you can subscribe to my weekly newsletter, Playing-It-Safe. Go to this website: www.thisisdoctorz.com/playing-it-safe-newsletter. Every Wednesday I share a single specialized and exclusive tip with all subscribers.

DOI: 10.4324/9781003083153-61

(2) Reminder: Make sure to download the FREE AUDIO GUIDE "ACT for perfectionism and high-achieving actions" from my personal website https://www.thisisdoctorz.com/act-for-perfectionism-and-high-achieving-behaviors/

Humble Request

If this book has been helpful to you and you believe that it has important skills for others, it would mean a lot to me if you leave a review on Amazon. Reviews are the metric that people use to evaluate a book's content and what Amazon uses to make a book visible to others who need it. Thank you in advance!

(click here to review it on Amazon: https://www.amazon.com/Acceptance-Commitment-Perfectionism-High-Achieving-Behaviors-dp-0367369222/dp/0367369222/ref=mt_other?_encoding=UTF8&me=&qid=1630350078)

Bonus Content

Download the FREE AUDIO GUIDE "ACT for perfectionism and high-achieving actions" from my personal website https://www.thisisdoctorz.com/act-for-perfectionism-and-high-achieving-behaviors/

Acknowledgments

I'm deeply indebted to the ACT community worldwide for all the ongoing contributions, support, and caring for behavioral science.

A big thank-you to every client I worked with, in one capacity or another. Our work together has been always an inspiration to create more compassionate and evidence-based resources for overachievers and overthinkers struggling with fear-based reactions. This book would not exist without the many back-and-forth conversations we had in our collaboration together. Thank you!

I have a huge amount of gratitude for Matthew, Russ, Geri, Deedee, Rob, Simret, Nate, Natasha, Crystal, Eunice, Chris, Rodrigo, Stuart, Justin, Jonny, Mike, and Brian for all your support, patience, and encouragement while writing this book. Thank you for always being there next to me every time I embark on a new project and torture you with all my random comments, questions, and arguments!

And lastly, thank you to every person that has been following my work over the years. Your emails, messages, and questions have been always a personal reminder to keep doing what matters.

Appendix

Online Classes With Dr. Z.

I created an online class that teaches hands-on Acceptance and Commitment skills for Perfectionism, Procrastination, and Imposter Syndrome.

More information: www.thisisdoctorz.com or https://www.thisisdoctorz.com/act-for-perfectionism-and-high-achieving-behaviors/

Books Written by Dr. Z.

- Zurita Ona, P. (2020, January). *Living beyond OCD: Using acceptance and commitment therapy and exposure skills.* London, UK: Routledge.
- Zurita Ona, P. (2019, December). *ACT workbook for teens with OCD: Unhook yourself and live life to the full.* London, UK: JKP.
- Zurita Ona, P. (2019). *ACT for borderline personality disorder: A flexible treatment plan for clients with emotion dysregulation.* Oakland, CA: New Harbinger.
- Zurita Ona, P. (2018, August). *Escaping the emotional roller coaster: Acceptance and commitment therapy for the emotionally sensitive.* Chatswood, Australia: Exisle Publishing.
- Zurita Ona, P. (2017, July). *Parenting a troubled teen: Deal with intense emotions and stop conflict using acceptance and commitment therapy.* Oakland, CA: New Harbinger.
- McKay, M., Fanning, P., & Zurita Ona, P. (2011, July). *Mind and emotions.* Oakland, CA: New Harbinger.

Working With Dr. Z.

I love working with overachievers and overthinkers to get them unstuck from worries, fears, anxieties, obsessions, perfectionism, procrastination, and ineffective playing-it-safe actions.

A key question to my work is, "How can we get unstuck from ineffective playing-it-safe moves so we can live a meaningful, fulfilling, and purposeful life?" To answer that question, I do my best to share skills and principles derived from behavioral science – Acceptance and Commitment Therapy, social psychology, and organizational psychology – in a way that is uncomplicated, unpretentious, and as real as it gets.

You can work with me individually in two ways: (1) therapy or (2) coaching.

If you're interested in therapy or coaching, go to this website: www.eastbaybehaviortherapycenter.com.

Professional Consultation With Dr. Z.

I offer ongoing consultation to professionals interested in learning the applications of ACT for specific struggles such as perfectionism, procrastination, OCD, anxiety, trauma, and emotion regulation.

More information: www.thisisdoctorz.com

Speaking Engagements With Dr. Z.

I love giving presentations that are jargon-free, full of hands-on skills to put into action right away, and with many insights from current behavioral science and social psychology. The overall frame of my presentations can be summarized as "less talking, more practicing, and more living."

More information: www.thisisdoctorz.com

References

Agassi, A. (2010). *Open*. London, England: Harper Collins.

Atkins, A. (2016, June 21). *George RR Martin and Stephen King*. YouTube. Retrieved from www.youtube.com/watch?v=v_PBqSPNTfg

Baumeister, R. F., Campbell, J. D., Krueger, J. I., & Vohs, K. D. (2003). Does high self-esteem cause better performance, interpersonal success, happiness, or healthier lifestyles? *Psychological Science in the Public Interest, 4*(1), 1–44.

Besser, A., Flett, G., & Hewitt, P. (2010). Perfectionistic self-presentation and trait perfectionism in social problem-solving ability and depressive symptoms. *Journal of Applied Social Psychology, 40*(8), 2121–2154.

Blacklege, J., & Ciarocchi, J. (2006). *Personal values questionnaire: Association for contextual behavioral science*. Contextual Science.org. Retrieved from https://contextualscience.org/personal_values_questionnaire

Commaandco. (2018, August 25). *Writing his first movie script: Sylvester Stallone*. Retrieved from https://commaand.co/2018/08/25/writing-his-first-movie-script-sylvester-stallone/

Costa, P. T. (1993). *Personality disorders and the five-factor model of personality* (2nd ed.). Washington, DC: American Psychological Association.

Duckworth, A. (2016). *Grit: The power of passion and perseverance*. New York: Scribner.

Fixler, K. (2012). Shooting for perfection basketball legend Rick Barry was virtually flawless shooting the underhand free throw. Why won't anyone give it a try? Retrieved from https://www.sbnation.com/longform/2012/12/13/3758698/rick-barry-underhand-free-throw-nba

Flett, G. L., Greene, A., & Hewitt, P. L. (2004). Dimensions of perfectionism and anxiety sensitivity. *Journal of Rational-Emotive and Cognitive-Behavior Therapy, 22*(1), 39–57.

Godin, S. (2007). *The dip: A little book that teaches you when to quit and when to stick*. New York: Portfolio.

Hewitt, P. L., & Flett, G. L. (1993). Dimensions of perfectionism, daily stress, and depression: A test of the specific vulnerability hypothesis. *Journal of Abnormal Psychology, 102*(1), 58.

King, P. (2018). *The science of overcoming procrastination: How to be disciplined, break inertia, manage your time, and be productive. Get off your butt and get things done!* Scotts Valley, CA: Createspace Independent Publishing Platform.

Kruglanski, A. W., & Webster, D. M. (1996). Motivated closing of the mind: "Seizing" and "freezing". *Psychological Review, 103,* 263–283.

Mueller, C. M., & Dweck, C. S. (1998). Praise for intelligence can undermine children's motivation and performance. *Journal of Personality and Social Psychology, 75*(1), 33–52.

Pavlina, S. (2015, December 2). *Plodding and bursting – Steve Pavlina.* Steve Pavlina – Personal Development for Smart People. Retrieved from https://stevepavlina.com/blog/2012/10/plodding-and-bursting/

Schwantes, M. (2018). *3 Things Wharton's Adam Grant says you should do to be truly successful.* Inc. Retrieved from https://www.inc.com/marcel-schwantes/3-things-whartons-adam-grant-says-you-should-do-to-be-truly-successful.html

Schwartz, B. (2004). *The paradox of choice: why more is less.* New York: Harper Perennial. (Rick Barry, in an interview with 2012).

World Economic Forum. (2020). *This is how COVID-19 could change the world of work for good.* Retrieved from www.weforum.org/agenda/2020/04/here-s-how-coronavirus-has-changed-the-world-of-work-covid19-adam-grant/

Yang, M.-L., & Chiou, W. B. (2010). Looking online for the best romantic partner reduces decision quality: The moderating role of choice-making strategies. *Cyberpsychology, Behavior, and Social Networking, 13*(2).

Zurita Ona, P. (2018). *Escaping the emotional roller coaster: ACT for the emotionally sensitive.* Chatswood, Australia: Exisle Publishing.

Printed in Great Britain
by Amazon